Rebels In Time

Rebels In Time

Three Plays by
Ken Mitchell

Hi Bonnie,

Ken "Bethune" Mitchell

NeWest Press
Edmonton

Edited by Don Kerr and Diane Bessai
Prairie Play Series: 10
Series Editor, Diane Bessai

Bella Pomer c/o Bella Pomer Agency Inc.,
22 Shallmar Blvd, Toronto, Canada, M5N 2Z8

First Edition

Canadian Cataloguing in Publication Data

Mitchell, Ken, 1940-
Rebels In Time

Contents: Gone the burning sun - Davin, the politician - The great cultural revolution.
ISBN 0-920897-05-3

1. Bethune, Norman - Drama. 2. Davin, Nicholas Flood, 1843-1901 - Drama. 3. Wu, Han, 1909-. Hai Jui pa kuan - Drama. I. Title.
PS8576.I88R4 1991 C812'.54 C91-091467-2
PR9199.3.M57R4 1991

(Prairie Play Series Number 10)

NeWest Press gratefully acknowledges the financial assistance of Alberta Culture and Multiculturalism, The Alberta Foundation for the Literary Arts, The Canada Council, The NeWest Institute for Western Canadian Studies, and the Saskatchewan Arts Board.

Printed and bound in Canada by Kromar Printing Ltd., Winnipeg

NeWest Publishers Limited
#310, 10359-82 Avenue
Edmonton, Alberta T6E 1Z9

Credits
COVER & INTERIOR DESIGN: Bob Young/BOOKENDS DESIGNWORKS
COVER PHOTOGRAPH: Spyro Egarhos
PHOTOGRAPHS: *Davin: The Politician*: The Globe Theatre; *Gone the Burning Sun*: John MacDonald; *The Great Cultural Revolution*: The Vancouver Sun.

The author wishes to acknowledge the continuing generous assistance of the University of Regina, the Saskatchewan Arts Board, and the Canada Council in the development of these dramas. Also noteworthy were Saskatchewan Playwrights Workshop, Montreal Playwrights Workshop, and the New Play Centre of Vancouver.

For My Uncle, Alex Mitchell

Contents

Editor's Introduction

These three plays are Ken Mitchell at his best, writing the world he's made particularly his own, the world of heroes. That's even the name of his first play, written twenty years ago and first performed in 1972. He's been a prolific dramatist ever since, but these new plays also take the form of tragedy. The heroes, Nicholas Flood Davin, Norman Bethune and Wu Han, all chose their own life, against the dictates of safety, and they act on life as much as it does on them. Indeed, except for Davin and his diminished end, the heroes gain their apotheosis in defeat or death. Writing tragedies today requires a nice balancing act, between a language which is realistic and yet condensed and heightened, between the everyday and myth, and in Mitchell's case between faith to history and faith to story. Mitchell finds those balances and it's an important achievement to have situated our heroes in the great tradition of tragedy.

All three plays have been published before and all are revised by Mitchell for this edition. *Davin: The Politician* was the second volume in the NeWest Play Series, in 1979, and this volume the tenth in the series. The play has long been out of print. In this version Mitchell has added the framing story of Davin's daughter, from the première production, partly to mute the suddenness of that final gunshot, and has pruned dialogue throughout, though the scenes and their order remain the same. It is more playable in this version. *Gone the Burning Sun* was published by Playwrights Canada in 1984 and while the play has held its basic scene structure both before and after that edition it has undergone numerous transformations in language and emphasis, partly to accommodate different performers in this one-man play, one of whom is better at the public, political Bethune, another at the private, more emotionally vulnerable Bethune, and so on. There are many small revisions between the previously published and this version of the play. *The Great Cultural Revolution* was published by Playwrights Canada in 1980. Mitchell has here changed a two act to a three act play, retaining intact the play-within-the-play, *Hai Rui's Dismissal*, but condensing the political debate that surrounds it, so the play is shorter and more sharply focused.

These substantial revisions point to an important characteristic of Mitchell's plays. They are all in transition. *Gone the Burning Sun* has been transmuting endlessly because it has, since 1984, constantly been in production. It is, I think, his best play, partly because of the potency of the Bethune story, that draws into itself so many powerful kinds of lives lived on the edge, and then because Mitchell has condensed the story into a shape that is tight enough to hold meaning yet expansive enough for an audience to live the Bethune myth, and because his language is strong. You might think that here if anywhere the text would hold, after so many productions and with such success and quality, but even this version is I expect not the last.

We publish these texts by Ken Mitchell for reading and study, but the play's the thing. These very readable plays are really scripts for production and their journey as texts is only interrupted here.

Don Kerr

Playwright's Preface

I have always been fascinated by rebels, and I'm not sure why. I wasn't aware of it until critics pointed out a common theme in my work: the outsider's struggle for justice, often as a speaker for the oppressed, an anti-hero. The initial reference was to the hero of *The Shipbuilder*, an epic drama of the Great Plains, based on a true story.

But I've also dramatized the lives of Norman Bethune, Gabriel Dumont, Nicholas Davin, Tommy Douglas, Archie Belaney, Pere Athol Murray, Wu Han, Sitting Bull, all historical figures. And the same streak extends to many of my fictional heroes, too, like *Wandering Rafferty* and William Gallagher, the "Grandad" of "The Great Electrical Revolution." The latter is a wee Dubliner who challenges God, monopoly capitalism, and the Great Depression – a Catholic in an Orange universe, a blaspheming, indomitable terrier of a man.

These men have many common traits. Most were Saskatchewanians, and this may say something of the character of the province, or of the Prairies – where such extremists and "disturbers of the excrement" are not only revered but fairly common. Their ranks would also include, no doubt, Louis Riel, John Diefenbaker, and my Uncle Alex.

And they are men. There is no getting around this gendercentric view of the universe – or that such feisty and defiant attitudes toward the world – are summed up as "male behavior." One exception is Nora Cross, the hero of my musical *Chatauqua Girl*, a woman who virtually created Chatauqua in the West during the 1920s. And I am working on a play about Kate Simpson Hayes, the West's first feminist, a poet and author, who founded Regina's cultural and literary life. She was also Nicholas Flood Davin's lover, and was written out of history for many of the same reasons he was – but you will meet her later in this book.

Putting this contentious and short-fused collection of individuals into one book would offer a terrifying perspective on Saskatchewan character, perhaps even call my own stability into question. But the three plays Don Kerr and I have chosen show a certain balance. A trinity if you will. For one thing, the stories unfold on three different continents. (Have you read the book about the Irishman, the Canadian and the Chinaman?)

Yet there is also a thematic and structural uniformity. Each of the plays is tragic; a great person is brought down by a flaw of character, a flaw which is the extremity of his greatest strength: Davin's ambition, Bethune's pride, Wu Han's righteousness.

Ken Mitchell

Davin: The Politician

Playwright's Introduction: N.F. Davin

Biography and drama have known a long and cantankerous relationship, at least since the time of Aeschylus and Aristophanes. While the biographer's account is usually restricted to the proven, that is to publicly documented, historical facts, the dramatist re-arranges and even alters those "facts" to convey the story to an audience. The historian resents the story-teller's loose way with "the truth," while the dramatist is contemptuous of surface details which stand in the way of a powerful story.

Some selection of fact is clearly necessary in a two-hour dramatization of a life story. In this, the playwright and biographer face the same problem: how much detail to include. The biographer by nature is inclusive, but he or she must exclude the undocumented – the intuited or merely suspected. Yet that's the very material the story-teller is going to seize upon when tracking the character's "inner story," the psychological truths that are of such unlimited fascination to twentieth century Western civilization.

Another key difference is the format of presentation. Biographies are primarily prose narratives, and make limited use of verbal dialogue. The most orthodox won't even engage in speculation on what the subject "might have said" or "was likely to have said." Quotation will be restricted to interviews or published statements. And even in quoting, the biographer must decide whether to correct the syntax, grammar or punctuation of the speaker.

But a play is primarily dialogue. In that sense alone, almost every word in an historical drama is invention. And while historical drama traffics in invention, it is, paradoxically, a much more rigid form than history. It is structured by conflict, and shaped by a series of accelerating crises to a climax which determines the characters' fate. It takes place in two hours, not 800 pages, and must adhere to basic rules of story-telling that will satisfy a critical audience.

A subject without conflict, a character without deep internal divisions, will not succeed as drama. Some biographies just won't work, unless the playwright resorts to wholesale creation. At the same time there is a clear limit to an audience's tolerance of historical inventions. Hollywood kept making the mistake of excess in the early film biographies. They were very popular, but few of these romanticized histories survive, striking us now as patently artificial and contrived. Yet many film biographies like *Gandhi* and *Chariots of Fire*, *Laurence of Arabia* and Abel Gance's *Napoleon* have become classics of cinematic literature.

A drama can only alter history to the degree the audience (and critics) will allow it. A play about important figures of recent times, say Mackenzie King or Sarah Bernhardt, that strayed from the known facts would be laughed off the stage. Historical drama is tricky, which is why many playwrights, not to say audiences, avoid the form altogether. So why are they written at all, and who is an appropriate subject?

Historians write books to share their insights with the public. A biographer offers us a life worth examining, either because the subject has intrinsic historical importance, or because the life is a model, positive or negative, for our times. Biographies or historical dramas can become Rorschach tests of our social psyche: in one period, a film like *Patton* will win critical acclaim; in another decade, a film like *Gandhi*. These characters become exemplars of social behavior, powerful reinforcements of cultural values – like the stories of Greek drama or the Mystery Plays of the Middle Ages.

The best subject of drama is not, of course, the most admirable person, the most successful politician, or the wisest individual, but the spectacular failure, or the fatally flawed victor. A great story hero is a person full of contradictions, public and private. The eccentric will prevail over the well-rounded conformist.

Take Nicholas Flood Davin. If you've never heard of Davin, I recommend the biography by Dr. C.B. Koester, *Mr. Davin, M.P.* After Thomas D'Arcy McGee, Davin is probably the most significant Irish immigrant to Canada. He was a poet, a journalist, and a politician, from the time of his arrival in Toronto in 1872 until his death in 1901. He was the original MP from Regina when the North West Territories were enfranchised, and published several books, as well as establishing *The Regina Leader*, a once-powerful journal in the territories.

Davin was a colourful, highly quoted public figure of his day, but until Dr. Koester's research and my two dramas in the 1970s, almost unknown in twentieth century Canada, even in Regina, where only a school bears his name. Local history is unkind to people who disturb community values, as Nicholas Davin did with his bravado, his reckless consumption of whiskey, his scandalous public affair with the West's first feminist and poet, Kate Simpson Hayes, and his various assaults on the North West Mounted Police and John A. Macdonald's Conservative government, of which he was a professed member.

My children have attended Davin School, and I once worked for *The Leader-Post*, but I was barely conscious of his name until I read Dr. Koester's research. Though couched in scholarly language and bristling with footnotes, it is a riveting account of a fascinating man, an Irishman born to dire poverty who educates himself, goes to London to study law and become a journalist during the Franco-Prussian War, decides to create a new identity in the Canadian colonies, and hurls himself at the windmills of life with the fevered intensity of a prophet creating a new utopia in the wilderness. The theme of his biography is one of metamorphosis, in which Davin sheds more skins than a Western rattlesnake.

Here is a new Canadian who defends the assassin of George Brown in the decade's most sensational murder trial, who nearly wins an impossible Orange seat for John A. Macdonald in Ontario, falls from grace, and sets out for the Great Lone Land on his fourth attempt (after Cork, London and Toronto) to re-invent himself. He arrives at the end of the railroad, the less-than-promising Pile of Bones, establishes a newspaper and founds the Western wing of the Conservative party.

Davin's ambition was nothing less than the creating of a civilization for the multitudes that were to follow, a utopia of prosperity and cultural vitality he envisioned in his speeches and publications. With his fundamental belief in the power of words, he was even more of a pioneer than the sod-busters and cowboys. Language has been a prerogative of the academies since Plato's *Republic*, but Davin found more resonance in the vast openness of the prairie landscape than he did in lecture halls of the big cities. It demanded a voice to rival God's, and an ego to match. Davin responded to the challenge.

Alas, Davin died in disgrace, a political outcast and a suicide, betrayed by the apprentice he had taken in hand, Walter Scott. Scott later became the founding premier of Saskatchewan before dying, some accounts say, in an insane asylum.

To squeeze such a life, with its many supporting characters, into a two-hour drama is a challenge. The most orthodox of historians will concede that some events must be compressed, minor players eliminated, and a few conversations invented. It is *possible* to dramatize a life using only historical documents – the so-called documentary dramas. But while these are sometimes interesting as historical education, they're often theatrically inert, and do not usually survive their first production. *The Trial of Louis Riel*, produced annually in Regina, is an interesting exception.

On the other hand, to completely *invent* a play about Davin, say a re-creation of his final day of life at the Clarendon Hotel in Winnipeg, would do the subject a disservice because it would exclude the epic sweep of Canadian history, and Davin's relationship to it.

The need for scrupulous historical accuracy becomes critical because drama – unlike comic books and television shows – is created for a university-educated audience, a literate élite, that small but significant ten per cent of the Canadian population which attends theatre, views Canadian films, and reads Canadian books. These are opinion-moulders, the people who determine cultural values. They're often well-read in history.

Nonetheless, the power of drama lies at the centre, within the characters, not amid the historical data. It is the playwright's responsibility to understand the historical character so thoroughly, and intuitively, that the surface details – place, date, season – point toward the essential truth, the discovery of character, and are not the centre of attention themselves. Character is revealed and understood through conflict, and that's why of the thousands of "important" men and women in Canadian history, only a handful will ever become the subject of good dramas. Davin, like Norman Bethune, Archie Belaney, Tommy Douglas, Gabriel Dumont, and Père Athol Murray – other characters I've portrayed in drama – was an eccentric, a person who stood out from the crowd like a Porsche in a used car lot.

I believe that my attraction to subjects like Davin must be political. It's part of my commitment to building an indigenous Canadian culture, that fragile net which is, in the final analysis, our only defence in the preservation of national sovereignty. And one of the reasons Davin appealed to me was that this was one of his visions as well.

In his prophetic article, "A National Literature," written 100 years ago, he acknowledged a debt to the language and culture of England and then said, "But this cannot supply all our needs. We have a national existence of our own. There is a Canada to be expressed; an eminence to be sought which we cannot reach without that which is to a people what the higher faculties of the mind are to a man."[1] In the conclusion, he proclaimed, "Only a national literature can raise a nation to perfect unity and single ardour and make possible a generous statesmanship independent of petty clamps, ignoble props, rising in grandeur above clouds of faction and even the storms of party, broad based upon a people's will and crowned by the clear approval of an enlightened opinion, whose purity and splendour are drawn not only from the past, but from the future as well – that future for which foresight works and whence genius draws its best inspiration."

Brave words to be uttered on the edge of space. Only a heroic person could say them. Davin was a rebel in his time, one of those peculiar men and women who resisted authority and rejected conformity, and were more often enemies of the state than the great statesmen we honour in history. Such models become necessary in a contemporary world where there are no heroes, only varying degrees of incompetence and villainy among our business, political and religious leaders. In such a world, the heroes of the past become vital necessities.

To dramatize the history of Davin, I began Act One with his beginnings in Regina, and decided to engage the historical characters that inhabitated that world: Kate Simpson Hayes, Walter Scott, Endo Saunders, John A. Macdonald, Louis Riel, and John Thompson, the Conservative Minister of Justice. The exception is "The Man From Moose Jaw," a fictitious figure who provides the opposition at political rallies – where there is always a Man From Moose Jaw.

Following the première production (at Regina's Globe Theatre in 1978) I renamed the Hon. John Thompson as Stanley Burroughs, a fictional person. The reason was simple: Thompson died in 1884, but I needed a political confidant for Davin throughout the play. To keep Thompson breathing until 1900 required too much historical distortion – though few Canadians even know that John Thompson was our fifth prime minister (and a fairly good one, though that wouldn't justify his inclusion either).

There is another character in the play even harder to define historically: the old woman who speaks the prologue. As Davin's apparent daughter, she illustrates the biographical dilemma. Is she a figment of imagination, or did Davin have a daughter, contrary to historical documentation? The archives say Davin was childless, but Dr. Koester's biography, published after the play was written, reveals that Davin had not one, but two, illegitimate children by Kate Hayes. The girl has no name, and her identity is shrouded by a footnote citing "personal correspondence in possession of the author."[2]

Documented or not, she is a necessary figure in the tragedy. The decision to include her was simple, compared with the political issues central to Davin's parliamentary career: the Second Homesteads Act and the infamous Manitoba Schools debate. Both of these were long and complex struggles that consumed thousands of hours of debate in the House of Commons, and pre-occupied Davin and his colleagues for several years. And they were needed in the play to demonstrate Davin's eternal conflict between party and constituency.

Davin was one of the first Western regionalists, and his electoral successes in three federal campaigns depended on his ability to represent the West in Ottawa. Naturally, this led to direct conflict with his own Conservative party – and to Davin cooling his heels on the back benches of Parliament for 14 years.

(The Act Three scene of Davin's phenomenal 1896 election victory, which he won by one vote, is not an invention. Only history could defend this kind of truth, for as drama it would be dismissed as melodramatic contrivance. Davin was in fact elected on the tie-breaking vote of the electoral returning officer.)

Political conflict drives the final two acts, and rather than invent other, let's say more colourful, issues such as capital punishment or women's emancipation, I undertook to simplify his historical issues into clearly understood lines of dramatic action.

The Manitoba School Question was the Meech Lake debate of the 1890s, dividing the country along religious and linguistic lines. The West, led by Manitoba, wanted to disallow French schools which had been guaranteed under the constitution. The

Conservative government was determined to resist, on constitutional grounds. Caught between his supporters and his leaders, between common sense and principle, Davin opted finally to go with his party on the crucial vote, and was pilloried by the opposition. He was labelled a traitor to the North-West, and his last-minute loyalty to the government still failed to get him into the cabinet.

The Second Homestead Issue was a less turbulent debate, but again typified Davin's political dilemma. The government had offered free second homesteads in the territories to certain immigrants, and then abandoned the program. Davin took it on himself to fight Macdonald's reversal, promising second homesteads to all his voters, and initiating not one but two private member's bills in this foolhardy campaign. He eventually won the case for certain groups of immigrants, but in the process alienated John A. and most of the cabinet over an issue the voters had forgotten before the next federal election.

In short, Davin had a strong if not always palatable set of principles. He was a "disturber of the excrement," and it's easy to imagine Davin leading the Western Reform Party.

Of course, I could be wrong about the kind of hero that our culture needs or deserves, but I am fascinated by this archetypal character: the rebel, the misfit, the Socratic bone who sticks in the craw of the establishment, a flamboyant eccentric radical who chooses to go down in flames, defying the Canadian blandness which normally prevails.

I believe these characters are beginning to define our cultural mythology, as witness the success of *Billy Bishop Goes to War*, the enduring dramatic legacy of Louis Riel and Gabriel Dumont, of Emily Carr and William Lyon Mackenzie. These figures, outcasts or failures in their own lifetime, have become our enduring icons, and it's not just because plays about them are better *written* than pieces about Mackenzie King, Frederick Banting, or John Diefenbaker. It's because their lives epitomize some quality we Canadians admire but don't condone: the odd person standing up to the mob, the nonconformist who carves life out of the precambrian rock rather than trudge along the well-beaten path.

Without question, Davin was a minor historical figure in politics. He never did make it to the cabinet. But more than any other man of his time he articulated the vision of the Canadian West, the peaceable kingdom. He believed this hostile geography would someday be home to symphony orchestras and Italian restaurants, that a thriving literature would root and bear fruit. He was a visionary, and like most of that rare breed, was bad-tempered, mercurial and contrary. He died disappointed, and no one saw the significance of Davin's life in the nineteenth century. Only now do we understand that his destiny was not in politics as he dreamed, and only marginally in literature and journalism. If anything, he was a lover. His great contribution was his life, that ball of flame that blazed out of Kilfinane to Cork, Dublin and London, and finally to Canada where it crashed to ground once again.

It wasn't Davin's substance that counted finally, it was his style.

---

1. N.F. Davin, "A National Literature," unpublished ms., Saskatchewan Archives (#SHS 14).
2. C.B. Koester, *Mr. Davin, M.P.* Saskatoon: Prairie Books, 1980.

Trudy Cameron as Kate Simpson Hayes, Adrian Pecknold as Nicholas Flood Davin, Globe Theatre, Regina, 1978.

First Performance

This play, originally entitled *The Politician*, was commissioned by the Globe Theatre and the City of Regina. It premièred at the Globe Theatre, Regina, on January 10, 1978 under the direction of Myra Benson with the following cast:

Nicholas Flood Davin – *Adrian Pecknold*
Kate Simpson Hayes – *Trudy Cameron*
Judge, Critic, Opposition Member, Desk Clerk
– *Bob Collins*
Walter Scott – *David Diamond*
Endo Saunders – *James Forsyth*
Newsboy, Guard, Salesman – *Bill Hugli*
Conductor, Riel – *David McCulley*
John Thompson – *Robert Buck*

Characters:

Nicholas Flood Davin: an Irish-Canadian
Endo Saunders: his assistant
Hon. Stanley Burroughs: federal Minister of Justice
Kate Simpson Hayes: Davin's lover, an early feminist
Walter Scott: Davin's protégé and, later, opponent
Louis Riel/John A. Macdonald: figures from the past
Moose Javian/Horsnall: Liberal opponents
An Old Woman.

Setting

ACT ONE: Regina, 1883-1887
ACT TWO: Ottawa/Regina, 1887-1895
ACT THREE: Regina/Ottawa/Winnipeg, 1896-1901

Act One

Scene One ∗

In the darkness, the distant sound of a steam locomotive. Light comes up on an old woman in modern dress. She carries an old ledger book full of clippings and photos.

Old Woman: My father's life was trains. Like so much of our history. You might think history is dull, but it's not. I should know. A famous person once said that those who don't learn from history are doomed to repeat it. It became my life's work. *Indicates book.* This is called "A Search for My Father." We never met. But I came to know him well. The story begins here – in Regina. You could claim it starts in Toronto. Or Ireland. But here in 1883 – when trains began to play their part – this city was a village of tents. . . .

Lights come up on a minimal set. There is the sound of voices, off, as Davin and Saunders approach. Davin speaks in a rich baritone, with a County Limerick accent, more pronounced when he is drunk and/or excited, as he is at this moment.

Davin: *Coming on.* Cold, lad? Ye call dis cowld? By Jayzuz, ye don't know wat cowld is till ye've stayed up all night wit a peat moss fyer, and the wind howlin' rain trew an open window, wit nuthin' to ate but potatoes and oatmeal. That woz Kilfinane in forty-seven, lad – and if ye'd bin there, ye'd call dis touch of frost a balmy spring!

Davin is flamboyantly dressed, about 45 years old, and carrying a bottle. Saunders is about twenty and poorly dressed. They both have winter clothing.

Saunders: I wasn't complainin', Mr. Davin! It was just small talk.

Davin: *Offended.* Small talk! Small talk! Endo my boy, if you are goin' to stick by me in this venture, you will have to abandon small talk to small people! Davin will eradicate small talk from our daily lexicon! Small talk has no place in a big land! Words are like coins – they'll get thin from overuse! *Sweeping gesture.* If we hope to change the face of this vast wilderness, we must become poets! Inspire the public imagination!

Sound of a train approaching.

Saunders: Well – train's comin' in, sir.

Davin: Did ye bring the papers?

Saunders holds up several copies of The Leader. *Davin gazes at it, in frank admiration.*

Davin: By God now, if that doesn't impress him! Are the others coming?

Saunders: I uh dunno –

Davin: What?

Saunders: Well, I knocked on their doors, but – it's five o'clock in the morning. The party just broke up three hours ago!

Davin: Bah. Pantywaists! Don't worry. Scarth will show up. And Scott. Let's have a gargle.

He takes a drink.

Davin: Now remember – It's not "Stan" and it's not "Hey you!" It's Mister Minister. *He hands the bottle to Saunders.*

Saunders: Mister Minister. Got it.

Davin: Over here! Quick!

Davin and Saunders stand at attention as Hon. Stanley Burroughs appears and descends onto the platform. He is a distinguished federal minister of justice. He looks around, confused and blinking. He has a bag in his hand.

Davin: Stanley!

He steps forward to take Burroughs' hand.

Burroughs: Nicholas! Good to see you! *He steps back and looks around again.* Is this it?

Davin: Yes, yes! This is "it." The great North-West Territories. You are standing on its capital!

Burroughs: My God.

Davin: Ahh – you should have seen it last fall! When I arrived, there was nothing!

Burroughs: What is there now? *He keeps edging back toward the train.*

Davin: Haha – you'll get over it. Look – downtown!

Burroughs: Those shacks? Tents?

Davin: A few tents! Half-a-dozen buildings. And one of them is your newspaper.

He presents the newspaper to Burroughs with a flourish.

Burroughs: The – *Leader*?

Davin: We ran the first copies last night – announcing your arrival!

Burroughs: *Looking.* Hmm.

Davin: The newsboys are hawking it in the streets now. *He gestures at Saunders.*

Saunders: Aww. *Into the darkness.* Getcher first *Regina Leader*! 'Tario 'lection results! Conservative Victory! First *Regina Leader*! Justice arrives in Territories!

Davin: Endo – meet the Honourable Stanley Burroughs, federal Minister of Justice! Endo Saunders, one of our employees, my assistant – recently from Toronto.

Saunders juggles bottles as Burroughs shakes his hand. Davin nudges him.

Saunders: Hiya, Stanley.

Sound of train leaving the station. It fades out through the scene.

Voice of Conductor: *Off.* All aboard! Next stop – Moose Jaw!

Burroughs: There really is a – Moose Jaw?

Davin: *Chuckles.* Yes – the Liberal camp. Fifty miles west of here.

Burroughs: Well, you are making your mark, Nicholas – as I predicted. The paper looks good.

Davin: You are too generous. There would be no paper if it were not for you, and our great Party. Endo – a flask.

Saunders passes the bottle.

Burroughs: Nicholas – it's the middle of the night!

Davin: Six a.m.? The very hour for a toast! Endo, the cup. In this country – you take whiskey when it comes!

Burroughs : *Laughs.* As you say.

Davin pours him a cupful.

Burroughs: A toast?

Davin: *The Leader*!

Burroughs: The new banner of Conservatism!

All: *The Leader*!

They all drink.

Davin: And the national leader – Sir John A. Macdonald!

All: Sir John!

They all drink.

Saunders: Umm – to Toronto?

There is an embarrassed mumble. They drink.

Burroughs: Bit cold for March though, isn't it?

Saunders: Cold – you call dis cowld?

Davin: Endo – the bag. Come on – we have a stove blazing at *The Leader* office.

Saunders: I'm supposed to be a reporter.

Saunders takes Burroughs' bag, and they cross to The Leader *office, upstage left. Newspaper artifacts, a desk.*

Davin: Here you are, Stanley. Coziest office in the village. Our press is through there. A steam-driven Vicksburg.

Burroughs: The Old Man would like a few copies – delivered personally?

Davin: *Laughs.* They're gone. I sent a bundle on last night's train – special express. You think he'll be pleased?

Burroughs: I do. Everything looks first-rate.

Davin: And worth a thousand dollars of party funds?

Burroughs: Eighteen-hundred and change. Counting your "personal expenses."

Davin: It's worth five thousand at half the size! *The Toronto Globe* will be begging for mercy in weeks. If the Old Man backs us.

Burroughs: In new ventures, caution is a virtue.

Davin: Oh, spoken like a true Canadian! If Macdonald felt that, there would be no railroad! And no Territories, either!

Burroughs: Careful planning. Good connections.

Davin: Stanley, this territory is the future of the Conservative Party! And all ye trow us from Ottawa is crumbs!

Burroughs: *Irritated.* The party knows the value of North-West, Nicholas! It is *you* he is worried about.

Davin laughs. Saunders enters.

Saunders: The room is ready at the Criterion, Mr. Davin.

Davin: Endo – find this gentleman some breakfast!

Saunders: Mr. Davin, I, uh – have to write my –

Davin: Right away!

Saunders exits.

Burroughs: Solid young man.

Davin: Endo? Too thick! But he's ambitious. Only reason I took him on. If he listens to me, he'll be known as a founder of this city.

Burroughs: City? *Shakes his head.* The folk in Winnipeg don't think much of your frontier metropolis.

Davin: Oh yes – the Winnipeg papers had great fun with us. Pile of Bones. My reply.

Davin points to the newspaper.

Burroughs: "Regina - A Reply to the Philistines!" A poem?

Davin: *With Irish style.*

A pleasant city on a boundless plain
Around rich land where peace and plenty reign.
A legal camp – the province wisdom's home.

A rich cathedral – learning's splendid dome;
A teeming mart, wide streets, bright flowers,
A marble figure whence a fountain showers!

Burroughs laughs.

What city is this? A gentle princess famed.
For happy genius, it – Regina named!

Burroughs: "Cathedrals! Paved streets!"

Davin: The line is "wide streets," Stan – not paved.

Burroughs: *Chuckles.* Dear me, yes. *Steps to window, looks out.* The edge of nowhere.

Davin: There were other possibilities. Moose Jaw. You should ask Lieutenant-Governor Edgar Dewdney. He owned the land hereabouts.

Burroughs: Ahh – speculation!

Davin: Ha. Fraud, most call it. Anyway, Dewdney made his fortune from the North-West.

Burroughs: *Still looking.* A territory vaster than the continent of Europe – and a capital that looks like a pig-yard. Strange times, Nicholas.

Davin: With stranger to come. I tell you, this is the promised land! This pig-yard will one day feed the world's starving. We can create a new society – without five centuries of bloody war behind it. No religious feuds! No bloated aristocracy – a *tabula rasa.*

Burroughs: But with all these Indian and half-breed scares –

remember the outrages in Manitoba!

Saunders re-enters.

Saunders: They're fixing breakfast at the hotel now. Mr. Scarth and Mr. Watson are there, waiting.

Davin: A few local supporters would like to meet you over coffee.

Burroughs: And then – some rest?

Davin: Here's your schedule of speeches. Every major community in the territories. I'll go along, of course. Endo can mind the paper.

Saunders: Yes, sir!

Davin: You write up the minister's triumphant arrival. Here's the rest of the copy for next week.

Saunders: You bet!

Burroughs: Is it always this cold in March?

Davin: Cold? You call this cold? Last winter was cold! It was so cold our cow froze where she stood and we've been milking her for ice-cream ever since! *Pause.* You should be here when it thaws in the spring.

Burroughs: Lot of mud?

Davin: A sea of gumbo! Walk down South Railway in April, you pick up a homestead on one foot, *gestures* – and a pre-emption on the other.

They go out, as lights dim on Saunders, getting ready to work.

Scene Two * *

Lights come up on Kate Simpson in her Victorian parlour, upstage right. She is about 28, and very attractive.

Kate: Walter? We'll have the punch in here, Walter.

Walter Scott staggers under the weight of the punch bowl. He is about twenty but tries to appear older.

Kate: It was sweet of you to come early. Did you put up the notices?

Scott: Both hotels. And the barber shop.

Kate: Oh, I know we'll have a big turn-out. Did they put it in the paper?

Scott hands her The Leader.

Scott: Volume one, number one. P-page three.

Kate: *Reads.* "Founding meeting of the Regina Literary and Musical Society. In the salon of Mrs. Kate Simpson. Eight p.m. Wednesday. " Excellent." Oh, my God!

Scott: *Nervously.* Er, what?

Kate: This poem! Look! The fellow sticks one of his own abominable efforts on the front page! What a pompous boor!

Scott: I believe he's Irish, Mrs. Simpson.

Kate: Obviously! *Sighs.* We face a long, hard struggle for art in this town, Walter.

Scott: Oh. What if he – er, comes tonight?

Kate: Let him show his face!

Scott: *In pain.* Well – they were – drinking at the Criterion earlier and –

Kate: They?

Scott: Mr. Davin – the editor. And Mr. Burroughs, the federal Minister of Justice. They seemed interested in the music.

Kate: With the Bartlett sisters coming? There'll be a scandal! And that little Anglican priest – what's his name? – who writes sestinas.

Scott: Father Banting.

Davin, Burroughs and Saunders can be heard coming near. Davin is singing an Irish ballad, perhaps "The Wild Colonial Boy."

Kate: Oh, dear!

Scott: Perhaps that's them now.

Kate: Walter – try to get rid of them. Before the Bartletts arrive! If there's a scene, we'll never have a salon.

Scott: *Gallantly.* I'll try! *Starts to go out.*

Davin enters waving a silver whiskey flask.

Scott: Shh. Restrain yourself, Mr. Davin.

Davin: The minstrels have arrived!

Saunders attempts to carry on singing. Davin slaps a hand over his mouth.

Davin: Enough!

Burroughs: Good evening, Mr. Scott. Are we in time?

Saunders: Order me another red eye. Oops.

Scott: There is no liquor here. We have only light refreshment –

Burroughs: *To Scott.* But this is a public reading?

Scott: Yes.

Davin: Reading? More like a dirge! I'm already sorry we came. A lot of old prunes and Anglican ministers. I'll bet you a good cigar this Mrs. Simpson wears a hearing trumpet and a wooden leg! *Laughter.*

Kate suddenly appears.

Scott: Mister Davin! You are – forcing me to –

Kate: What is the meaning of this outrage?

Scott: Mrs. Simpson, these – gentlemen were just leaving.

Burroughs: Mrs. Simpson?

Davin turns, stunned.

Davin: The Muse of Poetry!

Kate: Walter, rid my house of these ruffians!

Scott: *Turning pale.* I-I-I-I –

Davin: Madam, this is the federal Minister of Justice!

Kate: Well, we have no illegal substance in our punch, sir. You may inspect it yourself.

Davin: Don't apologize for the punch, madam. We've brought our own "refreshment."

Kate: Oh yes, straight from the livery stable?

Burroughs: Mrs. Simpson, my friends have been enjoying the grape, but they don't mean to offend. Mr. Nicholas Flood Davin. His assistant, Endo Saunders. I am Stanley Burroughs.

Kate: I see. And you are musicians? Poets?

Saunders: Mister Davin is a poet! A great poet!

Kate: Well, you couldn't prove it by the crude parody he had to publish in his own newspaper!

Davin: *Shocked.* Pardon?

Kate: "Whence a fountain showers!" What are you advocating, Mr. Davin? Public urinals?

A shocked silence.

Now, if you have been sufficiently entertained for the evening, perhaps you will –

Burroughs: Of course – we did not intend to embarrass –

Davin: *Suddenly.* You are a poetess, Mrs. Simpson?

Kate: I am a poet, Mr. Davin.

Davin: Well, we have discussed my credentials, young lady. What are yours? I do not recall the name "Simpson" in the magazines.

Kate: Simpson is my husband's name, Mr. Davin – not mine. I use the name of Markwell.

Davin: *Stunned.* Markwell! Mary Markwell?

Kate: Yes. Now, you probably have some important gossip to write – and I am expecting guests –

Davin: But you sent your work to the newspaper! We are going to print it.

Kate: How delightful! I'm sure I'm grateful – to appear in such august company.

Davin: Don't bandy insults with me, young lady – !

Burroughs: Nicholas! We did not come to start a ruction!

Davin: What?

Burroughs: Let us leave before you embarrass us all.

Davin: Leave? But the party's just begun! No, I am now on my best behaviour. The parson shall be educated!

Burroughs: We have outstayed our welcome.

Davin: Nonsense. Davin is welcome everywhere in Regina! I put the question to Mrs. Simpson. Shall we form a truce for the cultivation of taste and imagination in this outpost of civilization? The mystic female of the muse and the journalist swine with his Pipes of Pan? I have a good voice, madam.

Kate: *Taken off guard.* Well – we cannot allow whiskey –

Davin: I hand the flask to my sword-bearer, who shall carry it from these sacred grounds. *Hands it to Saunders.*

Kate: *Remembering.* Good Lord, Reverend Banting will be here any minute!

Davin: "Then we shall tempt him lyrics sweet and rough to join our merry company."

Kate: Ah – Swinburne.

Davin: *Smiles.* No. Davin.

Kate: *Flustered.* Please. Promise not to be rude.

Davin: I swear on my dear sweet mother's grave.

Burroughs: And I.

Kate: If there is any enthusiasm, we could have a light opera by the summer. I've already spoken to the Mounted Police superintendent – and he's agreed to make his men take part.

Burroughs: Heavens. You'll have an opera house before the courthouse!

Kate: And why not? Mr. Burroughs! You can help!

Burroughs: Sorry, but – I am completely tone deaf. In any case, I leave for Ottawa tomorrow.

Kate: Even better. Raise it in cabinet! *Glances at Davin.* Please excuse me, the other guests . . . *She exits.*

Burroughs: Nicholas, Pile of Bones is already looking brighter. I hope you will cultivate this rose.

Davin: Nicholas Flood Davin, slave to the Muse of Poetry.

Davin begins to sing a Gilbert and Sullivan song, perhaps "Admiral of the Queen's Navy." Burroughs, Saunders and Scott join in. Gilbert and Sullivan music bridges.

Scene Three * * *

Lights come up on The Leader *office. Much activity: Davin and Saunders carrying proofs, page dummies, type, etc.*

Newsboy: *Off.* Rebellion in the West! Read it in *The Leader*! Half-breed rebellion! Louis Riel returns from exile!

Saunders: There's a headline to get attention, sir!

Davin: Aye, it'll sell newspapers! But will the government listen? It will take a full-scale war before Ottawa wakes up to the problem.

Saunders: A war? A real war?

Davin: Inevitable. Everyone's bitter – the half-breeds, settlers, even the Mounties! It's the thirteen colonies all over again.

Saunders: I might even be an officer. Corporal Endo Saunders.

Davin: On which side, Endo?

Kate flashes in, brightly dressed in a frock and hat.

Kate: Nicholas, may I interrupt?

Davin: Top o' the mornin', Katie my Kate!

Kate: *Laughing.* Only stage Irishmen talk like that.

Davin: Begorrah, bejabbers, and wot would be givin' ye that quaint notion?

They laugh.

Kate: Well. Are you coming to rehearsal tonight?

Davin: You couldn't keep me away with a herd of mustangs!

Kate: You've been too diligent, Mr. Davin. There must be an ulterior motive in your devotion.

Davin: Discovered, by God! I confess – I've been courting the Spinsters Bartlett!

Kate: You devil!

Davin: Could you not tell? Father Banting last week caught me in the act of reciting a poem to Enid Bartlett's buck teeth. She was writhing in ecstasy!

Saunders guffaws loudly.

Davin: All right Endo – go and set that ad for the butcher shop.

Right now!

Saunders goes out. A pause. Davin moves to kiss Kate.

Kate: Stop! Not here. What Father Banting must think!

Davin: Why, do you think he knows?

Kate: They all know.

Davin: And if they do? We are free and consenting adults. It's common knowledge you left your husband in Nova Scotia.

Kate: Yes, but – you have a position.

Davin: We both have a position.

Kate: You are involved in – politics. *Pause.* It's very public.

Davin: Have you considered re-marrying, Kate? You'll never go back to him.

Kate: *Turning away.* I prefer our conversations on art, Nicholas – or philosophy.

Davin: *Goes to her.* Very well then – is it religion?

Kate: Is what religion?

Davin: This modesty of yours.

Kate: Well. You are a Protestant. How can you talk of marriage? Who would marry us?

Davin: I understand all that – I lived among the Catholics.

Kate: I am not allowed to divorce and keep my faith. It is a purgatory no man will ever understand.

Davin: With time and effort, anything can be changed. That is politics.

Kate: *Shuddering.* I loathe politics!

Davin: Why? It is the only instrument of change you have. Only through politics can you alter the deplorable state of women.

Kate: Really? Then you are a hypocrite.

Davin: A hypocrite?

Kate: Calling yourself a poet. Doesn't poetry ever change things?

Davin: It is for appreciation – not for change.

Kate: We are contrary on every point, Nicholas. Will that make for a good marriage?

Davin: Dammit, I love poetry! I have three books published. I love Macaulay and Tennyson. I'm trained in law and journalism and social graces! What else do you want?

Kate: Oh, I don't know! Peace.

Davin: Kate, give me a chance! We never speak except in this office, or in the company of Father Banting and the bleeding bumbling – Bartletts! You never invite me to your house!

Kate: But I have children.

Davin: And I adore children! Both Elaine and Burke *like* me.

Kate: Very well. You may come on Sunday. For tea.

Davin: *Remembers.* Sunday?

Kate: Ah – yes. The day you recuperate from your Saturday night revels at the Criterion.

Davin: *Laughs.* No. Worse. I'll be going to Ottawa. Stanley has arranged a meeting with the Old Man.

Kate: So – politics again.

Davin: Why is politics so offensive to you?

Kate: It was a passion of my husband's.

Davin: I see. Conservative?

Kate: No – Liberal!

Davin: You see? That explains it!

Kate: *Laughs.* You are absurd. So – you're seeing the Prime Minister and can't come for tea.

Davin: We need democracy in the North-West. This local government is a sham!

Kate: Is it?

Davin: The North West Mounties are little more than a private army! Its officers preside in total ignorance of the law!

Kate: *Innocently.* Dear me – ignorance of the law! You haven't – done something, have you Nicholas!

Davin: Herchmer! He did it! The police superintendent is out to destroy me! Oh, I admit I had a flask of whiskey. Everyone carries one on the train!

Kate: I'm rarely without mine.

Davin: But for a leading territorial citizen to be arrested and fined fifty dollars for carrying liquor – on public business, it's –

Kate: Infamous!

Davin: Oh, there's worse! Tried to accuse me of "indecent exposure!" Of appearing half-naked in the aisle of the train. Kate – a damned curtain hook gave way – could have happened to anyone!

Kate: It happens to me all the time!

Davin: You're laughing at me.

Kate: Well – don't fear being laughed at, Nicholas, or you'll never succeed in poetry, or politics! I have some appointments. *She kisses him.* I'll see you at the rehearsal.

She goes out. Lights fade.

Scene Four * * * *

Sound of battle, guns firing, bugles, etc. Lights up on The Leader *office.*

Newsboy: *Off.* Riel rebellion crushed! Rebel chief captured! Charged with treason in Regina!

Saunders: *Running in.* Telegrams from Eastern papers, Mr. Davin! They all want special despatches!

Davin: *Writing furiously.* No special despatches. They can scalp it from *The Leader.*

Saunders: But these are dailies! They can't wait for our – !

Davin: Starting tomorrow, and for the duration of the trial, *The Leader* will publish a daily edition.

Saunders: Daily? We don't have staff!

Davin: My boy, I have written for some of the biggest newspapers in Europe. You and I can do it. This is – *news*!

Saunders: Yes sir.

Davin: The entire world will follow this trial. It could set the course of this country's history, Endo. The voice of the *Regina Leader* will echo on Fleet Street!

Saunders: I'll alert the pressman.

Davin: Right. And we need extra capital immediately. Take this appeal around to members of the Conservative Association . . . !

Saunders: Yes sir!

Saunders runs out. Lighting change.

Davin: *Writing.* July 23, 1885. First Day of the Riel Trial. Where three years ago the only sign of life was the trail of the buffalo, what do we see today? The highest expression of civilization – a court of law. Justice has been established in the Canadian West!

Lights up on courtroom.

Judge: Louis David Riel, you have heard the testimony of the various witnesses against you. Do you have anything to say on your behalf?

Riel: On the day of my birth, I was helpless. . . . The North-West is also my mother. It is my mother country. . . . I had a mission. . . . If I die, I will *not* be judged a lunatic! My liberty . . . my life are at your discretion.

Judge: Gentlemen of the jury, are you agreed upon your verdict? How say you, is the prisoner guilty or not guilty?

Chorus of Voices: Guilty!!!

Judge: Louis David Riel, you will be taken to the place appointed for your execution – and there be hanged by the neck until you are dead! May God have mercy on your soul!

Lights fade. Saunders runs in.

Saunders: Mr. Davin! Quebec is up in arms over Riel! The papers are all quoting your editorial recommending mercy for the traitor!

Davin: I am flattered.

Saunders: But all the Ontario papers are saying you should be hanged! They call you a Papist!

Davin: Good, good. Lots of controversy.

Saunders: But – but Mr. Burroughs said . . . ! His telegram told you to support the judgment!

Davin: *The Leader* is not a mouthpiece of Ottawa! I only said Riel deserved our admiration. And our sympathy. He will be hanged in two days. Surely we can allow him some dignity.

Saunders: *Chastened.* Yes sir. Do you have the article on the execution watch?

Davin: Tomorrow. Hold the run for eight hours. *Pause.* We shall conclude our coverage of Riel – with a personal interview of the man.

Saunders: In his cell? Colonel Herchmer has refused all interviews!

Davin: That dolt! *The Leader* will not be silenced by petty officials! It can be done – without the approval of that swaggering dictator!

Davin puts on a dark black coat and a cross. He holds up a bible to Saunders.

Davin: Je suis Père André. L'ancien confesseur. Oui?

Saunders: *Shocked.* Mr. Davin, you don't plan to – !

Davin hands him a paper.

Davin: If I am not back by midnight, print this in tomorrow's *Leader.* If I return, we will have the interview of the century!

They exit.

Scene Five * * * * *

In the darkness, a female voice sings: "Riel's song." Light comes up on Louis Riel, praying. A NWMP guard paces, off.

Voice: Quand je partis ma chère Henriette,
Tu n'avais pas encore quinze ans.
Ma sœur, tu n'étais que fillette
Aux premiers jours du doux printemps.
Après mes travaux politiques
Vu les malheurs du Canada,
Je suis venu vous voir en groupe
Chez mon ami Norman Gingras.

Ma soeur tu viens faire ta visite
Au commencement du mois d'août;
En te voyant, mon coeur palpite,
Ô ma soeur, je t'aime beaucoup;
Reçois de moi la bienvenue
Mon coeur t'embrasse en soupirant.
Lorsque mes yeux t'ont reconnue
C'etait les yeux d'un homme content.

Davin is heard off. He now wears, as well as a robe and hat, a false beard and a large silver crucifix.

Davin: Merci, merci. Père André – pour Monsieur Riel. L'ancien confesseur.

Davin enters the cell, downstage.

Davin: M'sieu Riel!

Riel turns in terror.

Riel: L'Ange du Mort!

Davin: No, no! Not the Angel of Death. *He approaches closer.* I am Nicholas Flood Davin. Of *The Leader* newspaper!

Riel: Pardon?

Davin: I've come to hear your final message to the world!

Riel: C'est possible?

Davin: Quick – any information you wish to convey?

Riel: Que peux-je dire?

Davin: Anything!

Riel: *Pause.* M'sieu, do you think me a lunatic?

Davin: No, of course not!

Riel: Then why did my counsel tell me to plead insanity? Even my Métis brothers said only a madman would forsake the Holy Roman Church!

Davin: You are not mad. I said so in my paper.

Riel: *Clasping his hand.* Your name is Davin? Have we met before? At Red River?

Davin: No.

Riel: Ah, so much work left undone! Can you help me escape?

Davin: No – I cannot. You are guilty of armed rebellion. The penalty is death. It's harsh, but without law there can be no civilization.

Riel: Civilization? What does civilization mean to us? We are half-savage!

Davin: We? You mean, the Métis?

Riel: No! Us! You and I! Métis – Irish. You call yourselves civilized? Why are you here? *Passionately.* I tell you, we must make our own laws! Here on the prairie. Separate from Canada.

Davin: You are loyal to the North-West?

Riel: Loyal to my people and my home! I was a politician too, you know! Three times elected to Parliament – for Macdonald's Conservatives! And they never let me sit.

Davin: Why not?

Riel: Because I am a prophet. A prophet for a new people. Indians and whites will meet and become one race – the Pacific and Atlantic – Europe and Asia! Right here – eh? A new breed of men. Plainsmen! We are extremists in this land of extremes. Can you take this message to your followers?

Davin: I will print anything from a prophet!

Riel: Then I say this, m'sieu, to the Prime Minister. He should not be surprised that it comes through a newspaper – for he is a creator of public words. This I say, Macdonald! Do not be carried away with the glory of power – for it passes like the snow! In the midst of your daily business, take a few moments for prayer – prepare yourself for death – and eternal judgement!

Riel has become very excited. The guard approaches.

Guard: *Off.* You there – Priest! What the devil's goin' on?

Davin: Rien, m'sieu. We are praying for God's blessing. *To Riel.* And me? What do you see for me?

Riel: For you, a long but turbulent life. Much success.

Davin: Success?

Riel: In politics.

Davin: Will I go as far as I desire?

Riel: Further, M'sieu Davin. That is your curse.

Davin: And how – how far – ?

Riel: *Laughs sharply.* You must excuse me, m'sieu. I am in the middle of prayer. I am being hanged in two days.

Guard: *Off.* That's all, Priest!

Davin: Maintenant, je pars, mon fils. Bon soir.

The cell door opens. He steps out

And God have mercy on you!

Riel: *Calling.* You also, brother – prepare! The Angel of Death hovers over you! Be on your guard!

Davin turns and stares, shocked, as light fades on Riel.

Newsboy: *Off.* Riel's last words from gaol! Interview by Nicholas Flood Davin! The rebel chief's last words!

Sound of a roll of snare drums. A pause, and the sound of the body falling through the trap, and a crowd issuing a collective gasp. Lighting effects.

SCENE SIX * * * * * *

Kate in her salon, troubled. She is preparing for a meeting of the literary society. Davin reads his newspaper to her.

Davin: "He was pale. Quite naturally, he was pale. On the eve of eternity, he showed the highest reason. He died with calm courage. He was a triumph of rationality over the mob of brutes who shouted so lewdly over his death – or the atheists who thought him crazy to give himself to prayer in his final moment. *With rhetorical flourish.* We have recorded that his death was just. Let us, sinful creatures that we are, rise to the grandeur of being his judges!" *To Kate.* Well, what do you think?

Kate: Think?

Davin: Of my Riel coverage!

Kate: Very competent, Nicholas.

Davin: Competent! A masterpiece of journalism!

Kate: Well, it is certainly the prime topic of public discussion. The whole town can talk of nothing but your interview. The Mounties are probably on their way to arrest you.

Davin: Let 'em come! That despot Herchmer will be gnawing on his own liver! It's too late now. Ha!

Kate: Nicholas, did you do this for revenge?

Davin: No – of course not. Riel left a deep impression on me. He was a man of – distinction! He had – vision.

Kate: *Sharply.* For God's sake, let him rest in peace!

Davin: Riel can never rest in peace! His soul will haunt the gallows long after this little town has become a mighty city!

Kate: And you shall be cursed by it. Because you are as responsible as that howling mob of Orangemen.

Davin: Kate, Kate – be reasonable. The man was convicted of treason! We must be civilized! Otherwise there would be no place for – literary tea parties!

Kate: That has nothing to do with it.

Davin: Spoken like a woman. How can we impose culture on the face of this vast expanse – if we do not have the rule of law?

Kate: Spoken like a lawyer! I don't know, Nicholas. The law hasn't done much for me. How did the Indians manage all those centuries?

Davin: *Shocked.* The Indians were – primitive.

Kate: So were the Celts.

Davin: My dear Kate – you must be careful of what you say in jest –

Kate: I know – bad politics. I am sorry.

Davin: Why are we quarrelling? What is the issue here?

Kate: You are carrying Riel's corpse to make your grand entry into the political arena. Do you deny it?

Davin: Yes, I deny it! Kate, life is a nightmare of unpleasant truths. It is my humble burden to inform the public.

Kate: Hogwash. You are stirring public controversy to win the Tory nomination.

Pause. He smiles with all his charm.

Davin: Come to my arms, my Katie, my Katie
An' come to my arms and kiss me again!
Drunken or sober here's to thee Katie!
And blest be the day I did it again.

He tries to kiss her. She pushes him away.

Kate: Scoundrel! *But she is pleased.* Now you'll tell me that you composed that for me?

Davin: I did! I did! It's called, "Here's to thee, Katie!"

Kate: Like the devil! It's called "Marry Hae I Been Teethin a Heckle!" And it was written by Robert Burns!

Davin: *With mock despair.* An unmasked plagiarist! Pass the sentence, Your Honour!

Kate: Very well. You must recite a poem at the reading.

Davin: Tonight? A reading, here?

Kate: Yes. In an hour.

Davin: I have another appointment at 8 p.m., unfortunately. The, um, Conservative Association.

Kate: I see. Like the last time.

Davin: Last time?

Kate: The last time your friends met at the Criterion. We had agreed to take the children to a concert.

Davin: I'm sorry. I forgot.

Kate: Then why are you here?

Davin: Well, I, er, came to see you.

Kate: *Icily.* How flattering.

Davin: Kate? Are the children home?

Kate: Nicholas, this has to stop. The physical –

Davin: You're afraid they'll find out?

Kate: I'm not worried about the children.

Davin: The public. You are afraid of a scandal.

Kate: It's too late for that. The gossip has begun. It's just that you – are courting me and . . .

Davin: You refuse to be courted?

She nods, unhappily.

Why, in God's name? I am the very model of discretion! I don't come prowling to your door in the middle of the night!

Never use your name in public. I've even tempered my taste for whiskey!

Kate: I do admire you, Nicholas. Perhaps it's love. But – I do not want to be married again.

Davin: Then to hell with marriage! We shall live together in open sin! Or whatever else your fat priest calls it. That's where the problem lies, isn't it? The church!

Kate: No. That's not it.

Davin: Is it me?

Kate: No – it's me, Nicholas. I cannot – accept domination. Ever again.

Davin: Domination? What the devil do you mean?

Kate: You can't understand it. You are a man – and a politician. You would be a good father – perhaps a good husband. But I – don't want a – husband.

Davin: Nonsense! I refuse to listen!

Kate: Yes – well, I'm delaying you. You have an important meeting to attend.

Davin: And you begrudge me this meeting?

Kate: Not at all. Go.

Davin: It is critical! We're selecting a Tory candidate for the election! The one picked will be the first to represent Assiniboia.

Kate: And you are determined to be the man.

Davin: People say I am the only one qualified.

Kate: And are you – the only one qualified?

Davin: *Indignantly.* Hardly for me to say!

Kate laughs aloud at his pomposity.

All right, yes, I am! Then as soon as that is cleared up – we can take ourselves to the mountains at Banff, for a long overdue holiday! A few snorts of that air will brighten you up.

Kate: I thought you had forgotten that dream.

Davin: I've been planning it for weeks!

Kate: Nicholas – I would dearly love to go away with you. But can't you see the difference between you planning a trip? And us?

Davin: Dammit all, woman! Must ye fight over everythin'?

Davin removes his flask and takes a drink.

Kate: I think we should end it. Before your career is ruined.

Davin: You doubt me! So to prove I have the highest intentions, I will not go and make my speech tonight. I will stay in the parlour and cavort with the bards! *Offers her the flask.* Drink?

Scott and Saunders arrive, arguing.

Saunders: He must be here! – I've searched all the hotels!

Scott: Try the livery stable?

Kate: The bards have arrived. Put away your flask.

Davin: Kate, for heaven's sake – !

Kate: *Flaring.* This is my house, Nicholas! You will do as I – !

Scott and Saunders enter.

Saunders: Mister Davin! I've been looking for an hour!

Scott: I smell whiskey!

Kate: Mr. Davin was on his way to the Conservative meeting, Endo. He has promised us a poem, before he leaves.

Scott: An ode to Macdonald, no doubt.

Davin: Kate has been praising your literary talent, Mr. Scott. I hope we will see some evidence.

Scott: Whenever you like. *Reaches for his jacket pocket.* I have several poems in hand –

Davin: If I enter the political arena, *The Leader* will need a managing editor.

Saunders: You're not givin' him the job!

Davin: We must be realistic, Endo. He has an education. Who else is there?

Saunders: He's a dam' Grit!

Davin: Well – that remains to be seen.

Kate: Walter, recite your new poem – about the West.

Scott prepares a formal pose and begins a dramatic recitation. Davin must control his reactions.

Scott: Let us go to the West – the far distant West!
The mountains beyond it lie covered with gold!
On east of those mountains there millions can rest,
Where railroads in motion they'll always behold.
Away to the West, the far distant West!
Away to the lands that are verdant and green!
Saskatchewan Valley has lands of the best
Where rivers run slowly the valleys between!

Davin: Admirable. The spirit, if not the syntax. We can discuss our proposition next week – when my position is clear.

Scott: *Flattered.* It's only fair to inform you that I am of the Liberal persuasion.

Davin: Davin's journal is open to all opinions. I will write editorials, of course.

Scott: Oh, of course. What do you think, Mrs. Simpson?

Kate: Do what you think best. Personally, I think the offer offensive.

Scott: *Crushed.* Oh. Why?

Kate: You are being cynically manipulated.

Scott: But I need real work! Sonnets don't provide an income.

Kate: He thought it happier to be dead –
To die for beauty than to live for bread.

Davin: *Wickedly.* Sounds familiar. Yours?

Kate: Emerson. Are you going to read?

Davin: A small birthday piece for next month, but – *he takes the poem from an inner pocket* – time will not wait. Endo, inform the association I'm on my way.

Saunders exits, protesting.

Endo: Don't see how he can let a dirty Grit walk into our office and . . .

Davin: "Augusta"

We met. How blithe my laughter rang,
And yours in sparkling billows,
And through the pearls and coral sang,
Beneath your eyelids' willows.

In the dusky night, each star was bright
As the eve it glowed on Adam.
I struck a match – lit my cigar,
"So, now I'll flirt with Madam."

And flirt we did, nor did I fear
The fire in those glancing eyes,
Would burn up all I then held dear,
Make light all things I prize.

Kate is moved.

Kate: Your craft is improving, Nicholas.

Davin: *Checks his watch.* My apologies to Father Banting, and the Bartlett Sisters. I will attend the next meeting – without fail!

Davin goes out. Lights fade.

Kate: Nicholas! Will you ever love a woman the way you love a crowd?

SCENE SEVEN * * * * * * *

Lights come up on a speaking platform, adorned with signs and posters. Saunders appears, handing out leaflets. The Moose Javian Liberal appears.

Moose Javian: Political meetin'?

Saunders: Conservative. Nicholas Davin. You know him?

Moose Javian: I'm no Tory, boy.

Saunders: Well, you have my word that he's the best man for Ottawa!

Moose Javian: And what's the word of a – Tory bootlick worth?

Saunders: Say, did you come here to cause a ruckus?

Moose Javian: I'm here to express my democratic opinion – bootlick!

Saunders: You filthy vagrant! I'll –

They square off as Burroughs enters.

Burroughs: Gentleman, gentlemen! Calm yourselves! We'll have a respectable meeting tonight! Last speech of the campaign!

Saunders: This son of a Grit came to stir up trouble!

Moose Javian: What? You stinkin' –

Burroughs: This man is a voter, Mr. Saunders – and his views are welcomed here. Are you from Regina, sir?

Moose Javian: *Very surly.* Moose Jaw.

Burroughs: Ah – from Moose Jaw! Davin will value *your* support.

Davin enters, with the confidence of a born winner. He wears a flower in his lapel, shakes hands all around. Burroughs follows him to the platform, then Saunders.

Saunders: Fellows! The Honourable Stanley Burroughs!

Burroughs: Gentlemen – I'm not going to waste your valuable time with Eastern flapdoodle. I am here to introduce the man destined to lead the western Conservatives! The man who will stand at John A's right hand – advising him on *your* issues! Assiniboia's first Member of Parliament! Mister – Nicholas – Flood – Davin!

Applause.

Davin: Thank you. My friends and fellow pioneers. I will not dredge up unpleasant topics from the past – like the recent rebellion . . .

Moose Javian: We should a topped you when we did Riel, Dogan!

Davin: . . . because Davin is a man of the future! And we need someone who can envision the future, not the past – someone who can help develop the great North-West to lead the world in progress! Agricultural progress, industrial progress, and social progress!

Moose Javian: Ya got a nose like the Pope's knuckle, Dogan!

Davin: Ah – I see – a bigot has joined the crowd. Must be a Liberal!

Moose Javian: Ahh – yeh damn Irish drunk!

Davin: What's more – this unrepentant Liberal is a – temperance man! He must be from *Moose Jaw*.

Laughter.

Like my unfortunate opponent, a religious crackpot – Mr. Ross should be compelled to keep his minions in their cages until election day!

Saunders: Give it to 'em, chief!

Applause.

Moose Javian: How about second homesteads?

Davin: Second homesteads? My stand is a matter of public record. Mr. Ross has nothing to say on the subject! Nor does his filthy rag – *The Regina Journal*. They believe second homsteads are too extravagant for us *pioneers*!

Burroughs is growing nervous.

Look! *Waving a* Journal. "Davin a traitor to North-West interests!"

Voices: Shame, shame!

Davin: Me – Nicholas Flood Davin! Well, let the Ross gang campaign in the gutter! We will stick to the issues! And to you – my misinformed, misguided, misconceived Liberal – I say this: A Tory government will provide second homesteads to every settler who came west believing he would get one!

Great applause. Burroughs is alarmed.

And I commit myself to the elimination of federal duties on lumber and farm implements!

Burroughs stands up to warn Davin.

Burroughs: Nicholas, that's against our policy.

Moose Javian: Bullshit! Who believes him?

Davin: My friends. That Liberal doesn't believe we can do it! Can we do it?

The crown erupts with a massive YES!!! Moose Javian slinks off in humiliation.

Electors of Assiniboia, do your duty on election day! Vote to bring great public works to the towns along John A. Macdonald's railroad! Medicine Hat, Maple Creek, Moose Jaw, and Regina! Vote against the Liberal plan to starve the ranchers and farmers! Vote for the man who won you *representation in Ottawa*! – vote Nicholas!

Crowd: Davin!

Davin: *Davin!*

Crowd: *Davin!*

Tumult. Davin's supporters lift him onto their shoulders and carry him off. Music: "Colonial Boy."

End of Act One

Act Two

Scene One ⁎

April, 1887. A set shows part of the House of Commons. The bell is chiming. The Prime Minister's bench is prominent. Davin appears with Burroughs, looking more refined: a grey suit and cutaway, black-ribboned eyeglasses.

Davin: Stanley, the Mounties' morale is at rock bottom. His enforcement of the law is a joke! He is a tyrant to the public.

Burroughs: Herchmer is a firm disciplinarian – what we need to control those ruffians he calls policemen.

They stop at Macdonald's desk.

Davin: I'd like to speak to the Old Man.

Burroughs: Soon. We've only been in session for a week.

Davin: Wasting our time on pomp and ritual!

Burroughs: Learn to cultivate patience, Nicholas. The first rule of politics. You want to advance? You will have a chance at caucus tomorrow.

Davin: I want a personal interview on urgent political business! I don't care to fawn over him at a caucus meeting.

Burroughs: So do a score of others. *He points to the top of the* *theatre.* Nicholas, your seat is up there. Don't abuse the protocol.

Davin: *Glancing.* A back bench? I don't enjoy heights.

Burroughs: *Laughs.* Good Lord! What did you expect? The Ministry of The Interior? On your first election?

Davin: I am not joking. I know my value to this government.

Burroughs: And it will be recognized! First you must prove yourself. Here, if your ego needs a boost!

He hands Davin a magazine.

Davin: *Grip?*

Burroughs: "The Coming Man. Will any new member be more closely watched than Mr. Nicholas Davin? He is an independent member who can in his own words – 'rise superior to party.'"

Davin: *Pause. He is pleased.* Well. Well!

Burroughs: Don't let it go to your head. They are trying to seed dissent.

Davin: Dissent?

Burroughs: *Grip's* a Liberal mouthpiece. Next, they'll urge you into the cabinet. Nicholas, you are a rebel. They know the Ontario party nearly disowned you in '78. There are some who will never forget that.

Davin: So he sent me West – to punish me.

Burroughs averts his eyes.

Burroughs: No! To build a new base of power for the party. It's a test. And now he's given me the job of guiding you through your freshman days.

Davin: You mean, keeping me in line.

Burroughs: *Shrugs.* If you prefer.

Davin: Stanley. I shall always remember your help. I am a man of the party – first and last. But – I also have a constituency to represent – and there is room for honest conflict.

Burroughs: That is inevitable. But such debate must be held in caucus. Our party is the ship of state – and the PM does not tolerate much rocking of the old boat.

Davin: I'll do what I can for the government, sir. I only ask the same in return.

Burroughs: Tell me why you want to see the Old Man.

Davin: *Removing papers from his jacket.* We need new courthouses immediately at Medicine Hat and Regina. There is no belief in justice served up in tavern or livery stable!

Burroughs: This is easily done, Nicholas. It's my responsibility, not the PM's. I assure you we already have the project under study.

Davin: I don't want a damned *study*! I want action! In the West action counts! You must understand that, if you want to hold the voters.

Burroughs: I'll do what I can. In the meantime, put a clamp on your tongue.

Davin: What about the Second Homesteads amendment?

Burroughs: That is the jurisdiction of Thomas White at Interior.

Davin: *Removes another bill.* White is a puppet of his department. I intend to present this amendment early in the session, with Macdonald's help.

Burroughs: Let me take it, and I'll help if at all possible.

Davin: *Putting it back.* That's not good enough, Stanley. If I could only talk to him –

Burroughs: This is Ottawa, not Regina. Without help, you'll never get anywhere.

A bell rings to call the house to order.

Burroughs: Here he comes. Now – get to your seat!

They go off.

Scene Two * *

The Leader *office. Saunders reads from* The Leader, *Scott and Kate listening.*

Saunders: "Davin captures Ontario! The new MP from Assiniboia, Nicholas Davin, swept into Owen Sound last night to the sound of great cheers. Mr. Davin spoke brilliantly in support of the French language in the West, flaying the Liberal's position. 'This question is a local one,' the fiery orator claimed. 'The decision should come from the North-West assembly, not by a federal Parliament dominated by Ontario.' In Grey County, where memories of Riel linger with bitterness, Mr. Davin's remarks were extremely courageous. 'Butchering French rights cannot be justified,' he thundered, 'no matter how few their numbers!' In an unexpected display of approval, the Orangemen of Owen Sound threw their caps in the air, roaring for more from the eloquent Mr. Davin."

Kate and Scott: More! More!

They laugh. A knock at the door. Saunders collects a telegram.

Saunders: Telegram for you. From Mister Davin!

Scott opens it, looks shocked.

Scott: "Kill Owen Sound speech."

Saunders: *Grabbing it.* "Blizzard stopped me from going."

Scott: "Hold for future use. Davin."

Saunders: Oh – no!

Scott and Kate: *Laughing.* More! More! More!

Lights fade.

Scene Three * * *

March 15, 1888. Davin is at his commons desk, as are Burroughs and Macdonald. Horsnall, a Liberal, is present.

Horsnall: Mr. Speaker!

Speaker: *Off.* Mr. Horsnall, the Member for Cumberland.

Horsnall: Mr. Speaker, my question is for either the Minister of the Interior, or the Prime Minister. What will happen to the farmers of Ontario when their farms and livelihoods are destroyed by the mass exodus of their working labour to the so-called free land in the Territories? This is useless land, Mr. Speaker, fit only for the Russians and Galicians who are swarming into the country like maggots to a dead dog. . . .

Burroughs: *Rising.* On a point of order, Mr. Speaker. The Honourable Member has strayed from the topic again to entertain us with his appalling bigotry!

Pounding of desks on government side. Sound effects.

Davin: Mr. Speaker! My question!

Speaker: *Off.* The Honourable Member from Assiniboia.

Davin: *Rising.* Mr. Speaker, I introduced a private bill almost a year ago seeking justice for those settlers who had a right to a second homestead! This is government policy! Even so, some members of this cabinet have spoken against this bill.

Pounding on opposition desks.

Horsnall: You give it to 'em, Paddy!

Davin: It is hypocritical of this government, Mr. Speaker, to help big business corporations like the CPR! Yet in the case of these poor homesteaders, we have a great man, *gesturing toward Macdonald*, using his power against them!

Macdonald goes rigid. Burroughs rises to go to Davin. Turmoil of noise.

My question is to the Prime Minister: when do we get the vote on Second Homesteads?

Macdonald: *Rising with clenched jaws.* That is the responsibility of the Honourable Minister of the Interior.

Davin: *Bounding up again.* A supplementary question, Mr. Speaker.

Speaker: *Off.* The Member from Assiniboia.

Davin: Mr. Speaker, why is Mr. White not here to answer these questions? Where is the Minister of the Interior? This department requires a man of action! Instead, we get an antique – dead wood. Still, he suits this cabinet.

Pandemonium of cheering from the opposition. Macdonald sits, feigning indifference.

Burroughs: Nicholas – sit down!

Davin: It is an antique cabinet!

Macdonald rises and stalks out, stiff with rage. Much shouting and pounding.

Horsnall: Davin for Prime Minister! Give 'em hell, Paddy!

Scene Four * * * *

Kate's parlour. Scott is reading from GRIP. *Kate is writing.*

Scott: "Mr. Grip once again salutes that erratic genius from Regina."

Kate: Oh-ho! *She reads.* "And our advice to the government is to give the country the benefit of his talents. Mr. Davin has often been wide the mark, but we forgive him all, in view of the refreshing episode during the Emigration debate."

Scott: From a Liberal paper!

Kate: Nicholas will never be satisfied until he's in the cabinet. I'm afraid *we've* seen the last of him.

Scott: Not a chance.

Kate: Why not?

Scott: Well – he's railing against his own government! They'll never take him.

Kate: Hmmm. *Pause.* I wonder if he'll be back for the summer? He *could* play the Lord High Everything Else.

Scott: I doubt it.

Kate: Why?

Scott: Well, you know. The social whirl in Ottawa. Endo heard at the Criterion a story about Nicholas performing a Red River jig at midnight in the caucus room!

Kate: *Laughs.* Oh no!

Scott: Apparently he finished by leaping onto the table and jigging down the centre from one end to the other – kicking bottles and plates at every step!

Kate: The devil! That's what happens if he neglects his poetry.

Scott: Well – he hasn't let up there either. He sent us a new manuscript. We're printing it next spring.

Kate: Oh! May I read them?

Scott: I'm afraid not – he specifically said that you were not to see them.

Kate: Oho. Planning a surprise, is he?

Scott: Anyway. How can you be interested? You said he couldn't write a poem for beans!

Kate: Oh well – opinions change.

Scott: *Irritated.* You also said you weren't going to ask about him any more!

Kate: I'm not that interested, really. Father Banting was asking.

Scott: Mrs. Simpson – Kate – Nicholas Davin is less than you deserve –

Kate: *Smiles.* Oh, Walter!

Scott: He's probably got a dozen women in Ottawa! And more in points in between.

Kate: If Nicholas is not promoted, do you think he'll give up politics?

Scott: Forget him, and lead your own life! Your poetry is known all over Canada! But does he ever notice? No! He is a – an Irish – cad!

Kate: *Smiling.* Be careful, Walter. This is a political town. And he is your employer.

Scott: I don't care. I'll tell him to his face, if he comes back!

Kate: Come now. Let's post the notices for the Dramatic Society.

They go out.

Scene Five * * * * *

Lights come up on House, recessed. It is February, 1889. Davin is alone.

Burroughs: *Entering.* Ah, Nicholas – good news! Tenders have been called for your new courthouses!

Davin: Thank you, Minister.

Burroughs: And your recommendation for the territorial librarian in Regina, a – Mrs. Hayes?

Davin: Kate. She is gone back to her maiden name.

Burroughs: I see. Well – the appointment has been approved, *pointedly*, though such positions are normally reserved for party members.

Davin: She has exceptional qualities, Stanley. She will do a good job. Now – I no doubt have some obligation?

Burroughs: *Smiles.* The Old Man would like your co-operation on the Second Homesteads. He will meet you before this afternoon's session.

Davin: At last!

Burroughs: You assume it will be pleasant?

Davin: A chat with the Old Man is always pleasant.

Burroughs: You *have* pleased him by your stand on the French-language controversy. Perhaps there is room for compromise.

Davin: I certainly hope so.

Burroughs. Nicholas, I know you have ambitions for White's portfolio – if not more – but I must tell you, you are using the wrong tactics if you want promotion.

Davin: Oh? What are the right tactics?

Burroughs: Demonstation of ability. Loyalty to the government.

Davin: Not loyalty to the electors?

Burroughs: Few cabinet ministers can satisfy both.

Macdonald enters, looking grim.

Burroughs: Good morning, Sir John.

Davin: Good morning, sir.

Macdonald: Hmph.

Macdonald sits down.

Burroughs: We were just discussing Davin's role in the Second Homesteads debate, sir.

Macdonald: I should think so. *He takes the paper from Burroughs.* We repealed Second Homesteads after great thought, Davin. It would have cost us a million acres of land. But we're prepared to evaluate these claims – and deal with the matter next session, as a government measure. Your bill to proceed now cannot be allowed.

Davin: Not allowed, sir? It shall be passed! I am committed by a public vow!

Macdonald: That is a great pity, because it is contrary to our policy. The idea was a failure, and you should admit that – as I had to. A failure.

Davin: That is just the point! It was not the failure of some poor Highland crofter who came here on the *promise* of a second homestead! Why should he suffer for your mistake, Sir John?

Burroughs: This debate will only benefit Blake – and the Reform Party!

Macdonald: Let me enlighten you, Davin. I hope I need only to explain it once. I deal harshly with rebels. Ask Riel. I trust that you will learn from example. You are not out wrestling buffaloes in the wilderness! You have already been passed over once for promotion and your bloody Irish stubbornnesss is doing you no good. Here you get what you want by compromise. Always by compromise.

Davin: Mr. Burroughs explained that, Sir John.

Macdonald: Well?

Davin: I am prepared to – soften my criticism. I will not speak out against the government – if you agree to allow the bill this session.

Long moment.

Macdonald: All right, Davin. It will go on the order paper. And stop attacking Herchmer of the Mounted Police.

Davin: But sir – Herchmer's not the government! He's a scoundrel. I want his activities investigated! My assistant is compiling a dossier on the man now!

Macdonald: That could be awkward. We are promoting him to commissioner.

Davin: What? *Burroughs nods.* I see. I shall have to reflect on this.

Macdonald: Do. And remember – there will be cabinet vacancies in the spring. Don't disappoint me. Now, we have a Privy Council meeting, Stanley. Good day, Davin.

Davin: Good day, sir.

Burroughs and Macdonald go out. Lights fade.

Scene Six * * * * * *

May, 1889. Scott is working at his Leader *desk. Sound of press, off. Saunders enters.*

Saunders: He's here! Where's the book?

Scott: Just in from the binders!

Saunders: The party had a brass band out at the station, and they marched him down to the office for a whiskey reception. Overwhelming vote of confidence for his stand on the homesteads. Next election will be a landslide!

Scott: Hmm? You'll be writing all this up for tomorrow's *Leader*?

Saunders: Sure! Today's out?

Scott: *Holding paper.* "Hero's return for Davin!"

Kate runs in, excited.

Kate: Is he here?

Saunders: On his way. He said to invite you for an announcement.

Kate: About the book! Do you have it?

Scott: Not till he arrives. He must unveil it himself, it seems.

Kate: The conceit! If that man went to a funeral, he'd insist on being the corpse!

Saunders: He'd steal the pulpit from the preacher!

Scott: I don't understand the excitement. You've read them all before, anyway.

Saunders: It will be the first book of literature published in the Territories!

Scott: Well. It has more political than literary value. There will be an election within the year. I believe our bald eagle is using the occasion to announce his candidacy.

Davin: *Entering*. Congratulations, Walter! You are showing an aptitude for political insight.

Kate: Nicholas!

Davin: Don't listen to this noodle, Katie, my Kate. I have come for one reason alone: to treat my jaded eyes to the sight of one wild prairie rose. *They embrace.* How are Enid Bartlett and the gang?

Kate: *Laughing*. As good as can be expected.

Davin: And your new position in the library?

Kate: It was very thoughtful of you, Nicholas. I'm enjoying it.

Davin: Endo – the champagne!

Saunders runs out.

Davin: So you've heard rumours of an election, Walter?

Scott: Rumours? I only quoted your last dispatch from Ottawa.

Davin: *The Leader* continues to grow?

Scott: Circulation's up. Quoted in Minneapolis last month.

Davin: Excellent. You will be a journalist yet, Walter.

Saunders comes in with an ice bucket and champagne. He pops it open.

And now – the book.

Scott turns and lifts a small blue book from a box. With a flourish, he hands it to Davin. Davin cracks it open expertly.

"Eos: An Epic of the Dawn."

Kate: *Reading.* "By Nicholas Flood Davin, MP."

Saunders: Oh! MP!

Davin pours the champagne.

Davin: To the Muse of Poetry, and the company of friends.

They toast except for Scott, who does not drink.

Kate: Well, must we beg you to read?

Davin: Here I am travelling with Eos, the Goddess of the Sunrise. *He finds the verse.*

We paused. The broad prairie lay hollowed out beneath.
"Monotonous," she cried, "yet like the sea."
I said: "it's beauty must be seen from earth,
Its dazzling, glowing skies all clear of cloud
And fervent with the sun-god's strongest beams
Or strewn with soft white pillows tier on tier. . . .
When large and yellow suns go down aflame
Mid tapestries immense of purple clouds
And continents of vapour, their vast hearts on fire!"

Applause.

Kate: Magnificent!

Davin: Thank you, my dear.

Scott: Congratulations. I am impressed.

Saunders: *Holding out his glass.* A red letter day, Mr. Davin!

Davin: And we shall celebrate it in style, Endo. *Filling glasses.* Long into the night. I also have an announcement.

Scott: Oh?

Davin: If Kate will allow me.

Kate: *Horrified.* What?

Davin: The songstress of Saskatchewan will soon be acclaimed around the world! I took the liberty of sending a few of your poems to London. *He presents a big volume.* In a collection called *Songs of the Great Dominion*! By my friend Lighthall.

Scott: Pulled a few strings, did you?

Davin: Not at all. The work spoke for itself.

Kate: And which one of yours?

Davin: In fact, my own poems were not included.

Kate: Oh, Nicholas – really!

Davin: They declared yours the better work. Congratulations.

Kate: Well, I hardly know what to say! I'm – it's – wonderful! Though I wish you'd consulted me – !

Davin: More ambrosia, Endo!

Scott: Now we're all published, except me.

Davin: Cheer up, Walter. You will soon have added responsibilities with *The Leader*.

Scott: You're not planning to retire!

Davin: Hardly. But I am being promoted to the cabinet.

Saunders: Yippee!

Kate: Oh.

Scott: I don't believe it!

Davin: It's true. White's incompetence has finally become obvious and he's resigned. Oh, he had to be removed before the election – or we wouldn't have stood a chance west of the Lakes.

Saunders: *Holding out his glass.* Great news, Mister Davin!

Kate: Yes, I'm pleased for you, Nicholas.

Davin: You mean it?

She turns away.

Scott: I expect you'll want to run this on tomorrow's front page?

Davin: Not to rush. Best wait for the official announcment, eh?

Scott: As you wish.

Davin: Next week. We'll banner the announcement on one, with an editorial inside, um, commending the government for appointing a Man of the North-West.

Scott: I'll spare no adverb.

Saunders: Big party at the club tonight, right, Mister Davin?

Davin: I think not, Endo. I've been hoping to spend some time with Kate. I see I must make a greater effort to court her!

Kate: I can't go with you, Nicholas. Not tonight.

Davin: No? Why not? Some pressing social engagement?

Kate: No, I just don't wish to. I don't like the way this has all been – arranged. The books – the cabinet appointment. Am I the spoils of victory?

Davin: *Embarrassed.* It may be our last chance, Kate.

Kate: No – we had that: our last chance.

Davin: What the devil is it now? Has that cursed priest been nagging at you again?

Kate: What I discuss with my priest is even more private than my relation with you. Which seems to become more public every day.

With a gesture, Scott begins edging Saunders out the door.

Davin: Kate – don't be difficult. I've come a long way, just to spend time with you. We could be married, if you'd but say the word.

Kate: And what word's that? Surrender?

Davin: It's very simple –

Kate: No, that's what it isn't – is simple. Hasn't politics taught you that nothing is simple?

Scott and Saunders reappear.

Saunders: Mr. Davin? Telegram from Ottawa.

Scott: It must be the cabinet announcement.

Davin: It is. From Burroughs!

Davin reads it in great excitement. He looks up, shocked.

Davin: Dewdney.

Scott: What?

Davin: *Reading it again, stunned.* They've given it to – Edgar – bloody – Dewdney – !

Saunders: My god, Mister Davin – that's terrible – you'd better sit down – !

Davin: *Pushing him away.* Get away from me!

He turns away from the group.

Davin: Jayzuz – Christ!

Kate: Nicholas – please explain – what's happened?

Davin: Edgar Dewdney – our former Governor – has been appointed Minister of the Interior. I've been shut out of the cabinet.

Kate: Oh.

Pause.

Scott: Well, let's look on the bright side.

Davin: Bright side?

Scott: Dewdney is – steady.

Davin: He is a scoundrel! Worse than White. A common swindler!

Scott: *Not backing down.* Some thought him a successful governor.

Davin: Successful, hell! He was a bureaucrat! Interior needs a man of action! A politician! *Bitterly.* And they hand it to him – the man who brought us the Riel Rebellion! God, what stupidity!

Scott: You must admit he knows the West!

Davin: Yes – like Napoleon knew Russia!

Saunders takes out a flask of whiskey and passes it to Davin.

Kate: Nicholas. Please sit down. Gentlemen?

Scott and Saunders exit.

Kate: I'm sure it was a great disappointment.

Davin: Disappointment? Kate – it was everything!

Kate: *Hugs him.* No. It was not everything. You have friends. Your health.

Davin: No. In politics – I'm finished.

Kate: Davin? Finished? Hardly.

Davin: It was in my grasp. Burroughs turned against me.

Kate: I don't think you can blame your friends either. It's your own fault. Yes, Nicholas. Your defiance. That – arrogance! Where do you get it?

Davin: *Ruefully.* From the Old Country, Kate. I couldn't leave it behind. Maybe I should have stayed in the Golden Vale of Kilfinane and fought it. Pride is my curse.

Kate sings "The Castle of Dromore" to soothe him.

Kate:
October winds lament around
The castle of Dromore.
Yet peace is in her lofty halls,
My dearest treasure's store.
Though autumn leaves may droop and die,
A bud of spring are you!
Sing hush-a-bye lul-la-loo lo-lan,
Sing hush-a-bye lul-la-loo.

Take time to thrive, my rose of hope
In the garden of Dromore.
Take heed, young eaglet,
Till your wings have feathers fit to soar.
A little rest and then the world
Is full of work to do.
Sing hush-a-bye lul-la-loo lo-lan,
Sing hush-a-bye lul-la-loo.

Pause. Davin looks at Kate.

Kate: You can do it, Nicholas. Run in the next election. They can't defeat you. As long as you have the people with you.

Lights fade as they go out, arm in arm.

Scene Seven * * * * * * *

Sound of train in the distance. Light comes up on Macdonald and Burroughs entering the house. Macdonald seems much older, leaning on a cane. September, 1890.

Macdonald: He actually refused to come for the opening of Parliament?

Burroughs: I'm afraid so, sir. He's due on today's train.

Macdonald: I knew he was a disguised Grit. Keep a close watch on him now, before he wrecks the National Policy, and the party with it.

Burroughs: I understand your concern, John. But he was elected on a Conservative platform –

Macdonald: Bah! So was Riel. Remember him?

Burroughs: We should never have sent Tweed up against him. It smacked of Yankee politics. Worked against us.

Macdonald: If the blackguard had stepped down after Dewdney's promotion – as you promised –

Burroughs: As I *warned*, Sir John. And now he'll be more unpredictable than ever.

Macdonald: Unpredictable? Nonsense. I can predict he'll betray us at every turn. And I hold you responsible!

Burroughs: Yes sir.

Davin rises at his desk, in full cry.

Davin: Yes, Mr. Speaker, the leaders of this government *should* turn their heads in shame! They bribed Tweed to run against me – that flabby mass of conceited mediocrity! But even Herchmer and his stooges couldn't stop Nicholas Flood Davin. Mr. Speaker, I demand a full investigation of the charges against that tinpot dictator in a red tunic – the Prime Minister's policeman!

Applause from opposition.

Macdonald: *Turns.* It's you we'll investigate – traitor!

Horsnall: Resign! Resign!

Davin: Mr. Speaker, if the frowns of the Right Honourable Gentleman hold any terror for him, it is only because of my great affection – for him. But I am not the Last Spike!

Macdonald sits fuming amid the laughter and catcalls of the opposition.

Davin: They say in the taverns and tabernacles of the land that Davin hates war, but loves a fight! If the Prime Minister wants to battle on the question of the national police – I am prepared to divide this House!

Delirious opposition approval. Macdonald slumps in his seat, ill. Burroughs helps him from the chamber. Lights dim.

Sound of tolling bells in mourning. Light comes up again, and Macdonald's seat is draped in black. Davin wears a black arm band.

Davin: Mr. Speaker, it would be uncharacteristic of Davin to stand silent on this occasion. Our leader's efforts ensured Canada's future. He leaves a heritage of strength and hope. May I offer a few words to – the Old Man.

> Child of love and power and fame he came,
> An Empire's sunshine on his classic brow;
> He sought to win a nation's loud acclaim –
> The mighty future's hope against the now.

Burroughs: A fine gesture, Nicholas. You did yourself proud.

Davin: 'Twas the least I could manage for the old souse.

Burroughs: Well – there'll be a few changes now, with Abbott taking the throne.

Davin: Changes? I doubt it. Abbott is a pawn. Even more indebted to the financiers than the Old Man was. The West will be ignored. And there's going to be trouble over this Manitoba Schools business.

Burroughs: *Nods.* The sword of Damocles. Which way to turn? Still, we have three years to deal with it. It'll take leadership.

Davin: Yes – leadership. So why didn't you stand against Abbott?

Burroughs: This country's not ready for a Catholic Prime Minister.

Davin: Well, I'd stick with you. Even if the rest bolted to Laurier and the Liberals.

Burroughs: Good man. I expect you'll be here long enough to make a charge for the throne yourself!

Davin: No. I'm getting old. It's twenty years since I came to Canada. What have I achieved? Nothing.

Burroughs: You are still bitter over Dewdney. Listen to me – heed the party whip and the rewards may still be yours.

Davin: The carrot and – the stick! Well, what would be a suitable reward, Stanley? The post office? No thank you. I prefer a bigger – challenge.

Burroughs: Indeed? Like this motion on tomorrow's order paper? *Removes a paper from his jacket.* Or is it your idea of a joke?

Davin: It's not a joke.

Burroughs: "Moved by Davin, that the voting franchise be extended to – women." *Pause.* Have you taken leave of your *senses*?

Davin: We are approaching a new century. A new era. Women will be in its avant-garde.

Burroughs: Then God preserve us all! You've been spending too much time with radicals like Mrs. Hayes. Don't expect any support from the government!

Davin: I will take support wherever I can find it. This will be a matter of principle – and a free vote.

Sound of commons hubbub.

Speaker's Voice: As mover, the Member from Assiniboia will be the final speaker on the motion.

Davin: Thank you, Mr. Speaker. If there is any question remaining in the minds of the honourable members, I may refer them to the great women of political history – women like our reigning monarch, Queen Victoria. And there was the Great Elizabeth, and Mary, Queen of Scots, women of genius as well as beauty. Maria Theresa, Catherine the Great. If these women could discharge the highest political duties of their time, why cannot all women be entrusted with the smallest – and greatest – political duty – the casting of a ballot?

Hornsall: No petticoat government!

Voices: Throw him out! Seditious nonsense! No women! Bloody suffragette!

Davin: *Shouting over.* What objections can you have – when you compare women to the parasites and rabble-rousers who serve now?

Davin is drowned out. He sinks to his seat as the light fades. Sound of a train.

SCENE EIGHT * * * * * * * *

Light up on Scott and Kate, beside Kate's bags. He is standing on a railroad platform.

Scott: You know your way around Winnipeg? I have to get back on the train in a few minutes –

Kate: Thank you, Walter. Thank you for coming with me.

Scott: It's the least I could do. *Pause.* How shall I break the news to – him?

Kate: I don't even want you to discuss it. Anyway, I have no right to bother him. He'd feel he'd have to leave Ottawa.

Scott: *With anger.* It is his damned duty!

Kate: It is not for either of us, Walter, to define Mr. Davin's duties! He has duties in Parliament. The women's vote is important!

Scott: But – at a time like this!

Kate: Oh, don't be so melodramatic. You make me sound helpless! How can women expect to be treated as equals – if we need a *man* to run and hold our hands at every minor crisis?

Scott: *Stiffly.* This is not a minor crisis.

Kate: *Gently.* And you are not me. *Pause.* The library was good enough to provide an extended vacation leave.

Scott: Vacation!

Kate: It's no lie that I need a rest.

Scott: And the children?

Kate: Three months won't ruin them. We have a good nanny. You could look in on them when you go back, Walter. I would appreciate it.

Walter: You sure you'll be all right?

Kate: Yes. I may look for a new job. Something in newspapers.

Walter: Really? Well – why didn't you say – ? Why didn't you tell me? I could have . . . !

Kate: No, Walter – not *The Leader*.

Scott: He will tear me limb from limb, if he finds out you left town to look for work.

Kate: Then tell him I have gone politicking. To gain the vote for women!

Conductor's Voice: All aboard!

They embrace.

Scott: And if I tell him the truth?

Kate: He is *not* to know. I want your promise, Walter.

Scott: I only promise to act in your best interest. Take care.

He exits.

Kate: Good-bye!

Train sound and lights fade.

SCENE NINE * * * * * * * * *

Lights up on Davin in Commons. Scott enters.

Davin: Walter! Thanks for coming. Everything's so hectic I just could not get away.

Scott: I assumed it was important.

Davin: How is Kate? And the children?

Scott: All fine.

Davin: And the paper? No problems?

Scott: Well – we are edging dangerously close to a profit. If you stay here one more month, the figures will be in the black.

They laugh.

Davin: That's *your* influence, Walter. True enterprising Liberalism! I am counting on you to take over.

Scott: I? Oh, – nonsense! I've no ambition – !

Davin: Relax, I know you are not working behind my back. *Pause.* I intend to sell you *The Leader*, Walter.

Scott: Me? You've turned down every publisher in the country. You said you'd *never* sell!

Davin: Ottawa is expensive. I am barely out of debt. I need more funds to – improve my position.

Scott: Position?

Davin: *Speaking confidentially.* The government is in chaos. Ever since Thompson died. Bowell can't last. Charles Tupper will make his bid soon. I may never get another chance.

Scott: I see.

Davin: And I will soon be married.

Scott: *Married*!

Davin: Yes, didn't I tell you? I am engaged to be married. That always requires a bit of cash.

Scott: *Married*? To whom?

Davin: Her name is Eliza Reid. *Scott is shocked speechless.* She is of a first-class Ottawa family. We will have the ceremony here, of course. Before the fall session.

Scott: But what of Kate Hayes?

Davin: *Stiffly.* That is between Kate and me.

Scott: *Pause.* She doesn't know of this?

Davin: No, she, er, broke off our relationship.

Scott: Indeed! When?

Davin: When I was last in Regina. Three months ago.

Scott: Liar!

Davin: I know what you are thinking! But I did not drop Kate. She dropped me! *Bitterly.* I would have married her a dozen times! She will never agree!

Scott: She loved you.

Davin: Then why does she have to be so independent? I was prepared to give up my career in politics!

Scott: Are you sure?

Davin: Well, I – I – of course I'm sure! *Long pause.* Burroughs says it's a necessity.

Scott: Marriage?

Davin: Miss Reid is a handsome young woman. She is well-considered in Ottawa circles, has some income. A good wife is indispensible to a political career.

Scott: You've calculated your campaign very thoroughly.

Davin: If I'm to be a politician – I must have a politician's wife.

Scott: Well. Is she – attracted to you?

Davin: Attracted? *Laughs.* Walter – every woman I've met was attracted to me. Except Enid Bartlett.

Scott: But you *are* – what? Sixty?

Davin: Fifty-five! And Miss Reid is 21. What of that?

Scott: Well, if you are determined – *He shakes his hand.* I wish you happiness.

Davin: Thank you, Walter. I still have a young man's ambition. And I need your help. If you decide to buy *The Leader*.

Scott: Well – name your price. I have no money, so I'll have to find backing.

Davin: Liberal backing?

Scott: Does that concern you?

Davin: Fundamentally. That is my price. Political support. This will be a tough election. The Manitoba Schools question.

Scott: *Shocked.* You can't support the government on that! Not after your stand on Western rights.

Davin: I will *never* vote for the legislation! Tell our readers. Never! The federal government is interfering with provincial rights. However, French in Manitoba is guaranteed by the constitution! And I will argue for a compromise from within – the cabinet.

Scott: Do you support the Manitoba Schools Bill – or not?

Davin: Yes. In principle. However, the French minority must be protected.

Scott: I cannot agree to this.

Davin: You must run my editorials until after the election. I remain as Parliamentary correspondent. Those are my conditions for selling *The Leader*! That is my price.

Scott: *Pause.* And the, uh, financial price?

Davin: Oh. Shall we say – four hundred?

Scott: *Staggered*. Four hundred? For everything?

Davin: Presses, building, equipment. Reputation.

Scott: But it's not enough! You're cheating yourself.

Davin: *Smiles*. Perhaps. I'm not a businessman, Walter. Just a politician. Is it a deal?

Scott: You have a deal, Mr. Davin.

They shake hands.

Davin: Well – you'll stay for this afternoon's session – I can get you a seat in Visitors'. It's colourful at question time.

Scott: Thank you, but I'm taking the train back tomorrow. And I want to buy some presents for Kate's children.

Davin: Oh yes. I expect you'll be seeing Kate? Would you be good enough to – tell her of – my marriage? I'd find it awkward.

Scott: I – can't – *Pause*.

Davin: Oh?

Scott: There is something – I don't know – how to tell you. I promised Kate –

Davin: Tell – ask her to write to me.

Scott: She's gone. Left Regina.

Davin: What? Where?

Scott: Winnipeg.

Davin: *Winnipeg*? Why?

Scott: To, uh – look for a job.

Davin: Don't be absurd!

Scott: And to – have a – child.

Davin reacts, shocked.

Davin: A child . . .

Scott: She told no one. Only me. It's a secret.

Davin: When – ?

Scott: Three months. Nicholas – you aren't to know.

Davin: This is – a shock.

Scott: There is nothing you can do. I only told you so you won't hurt her any more. *Don't* write a poem about it.

He goes out. Davin remains by himself, staring into space as the lights fade.

Davin: Thank you – Walter.

Light on Kate, isolated. She sings "Kate's lament."

Kate: When you left I thought my heart would die.
How could I live without your word and smile?
How meet the sorrow all alone? When you and I
Together long had planned and dreamed. The while
You held my hand the road of life was sweet
And thorns to roses turned beneath my feet.

The sun still circles and the clouds still drift.
Prairie blossoms bud and bloom and die.
Sunshine and rain falling through the clouds' rift,
Tears and gladness come as I pass by
The same old pathway where memories bide
And linger in my heart e'en though – you died.

The bell bongs six o'clock. Davin remains seated, staring, as the lights fade to black.

End of Act Two

Act Three

Scene One ⁎

In the darkness, sound of locomotive stopping. The lights go up on Davin, entering The Leader *office.*

Davin: Walter? Endo? Anyone here? Endo?

Saunders enters.

Saunders: Mr. Davin! Good to see you!

Davin: I just arrived. Where is everyone?

Saunders: It's Sunday, Mr. Davin.

Davin: In my day, we worked seven days a week!

Saunders: Yes, sir. Mr. Scott will be in around three.

Davin: Hmph. *Looks around.* What's the feeling on the Manitoba Schools?

Saunders: Well – some of our people are growing nervous. Did you get the, uh – ?

Davin: Yes, yes, I got their telegram. Don't they understand how complex this issue is?

Saunders: No sir. Guess not. How're things in Ottawa?

Davin: Bah. Seven ministers resigned! Government is on the verge of collapse. I don't think Bowell can last another month.

Saunders: Sounds bad.

Davin: Tupper will probably step in and try to get us through the election. *Pause.* He'll ask me into the cabinet.

Saunders: Wouldn't that be great?

Davin: Not so great. If we don't get this language issue resolved, the Tory party will be dead west of Toronto.

Saunders: But you – voted for French!

Davin: Davin will never betray the West! I will not support separate schools! It is absurd! Tell all our people that.

Saunders: We'll call a meeting for tomorrow.

Davin: However, we can't be dogmatic. The constitution must be upheld. It's the only way to preserve Confederation. Language rights *must* be guaranteed.

Saunders: Oh.

Davin: We cannot give in to this baying for blood from every damned bigot in the country. We can have French schools in the West, if Ottawa would only leave us to do it, *our way.*

Scott enters, with brief case.

Scott: Nicholas!

Davin: Walter.

Scott: Come to repair a few fences?

Davin: *Laughs.* You might say that. How are you?

Scott: Well enough. *They shake hands formally.* You and – Mrs. Davin?

Davin: The same. My wife had to stay in Ottawa, unfortunately. Social obligations. How is the paper?

Scott: Surviving.

Davin: Oh?

Scott: Nicholas, it turns my stomach to have to print the propaganda you've been sending from Ottawa!

Davin: I see.

Scott: What are you up to? Nobody wants French shoved down their throats! Nobody out here wants schools run by the Catholic Church!

Davin: Neither do I. But it's more complicated than –

Scott. All I know is the equivocation you issue from the Press Gallery.

Davin: See here – !

Scott: I warn you, Nicholas – if you vote with the government to crush The Manitoba Bill, our deal is off!

Davin: Then you don't know much about the law, my young friend. We have a legal contract stating that the editorial control of this paper is mine! *Pause.* Now, this is a sensitive issue out here. But this much I learned from Riel: no one suppresses Western interests without a fight.

Saunders: Let's get this association meeting organized, Mr. Davin.

Davin: Right. The election will be called within weeks – and we need every Tory soldier we can muster! *They go out.* Keep calm, Walter – act foolishly and you could lose everything.

Scott, alone, slams his brief case onto the desk. Lights fade.

SCENE TWO * *

Lights up on a political rally. Saunders hangs up "Davin in '96" posters and bunting. Moose Javian appears.

Moose Javian: Howdo.

Saunders: You!

Moose Javian: Where's that traitor Davin?

Saunders: He'll be speaking shortly.

Moose Javian: Good. I'm looking forward to it.

Burroughs enters, supporting Davin, who is tipsy.

Look! He's blind drunk!

Davin: I am not drunk, shir.

Not drunk is he who from the floor,
Can rise alone and still drink more;
But drunk is he, who prostrate lies,
Without the power to drink or rise.

Laughter and cheering. Davin waves, ascends to platform.

Burroughs: Once more, I introduce my friend Nicholas Davin.

Moose Javian: Boooo!

Burroughs: His experience is *needed* in Ottawa – !

Moose Javian: Well, we don't need it here! Hahaha!

Burroughs: Send a Conservative to maintain the prosperity brought to you by John A. Macdonald and the CPR.

Moose Javian: Damn the CPR!

Burroughs: Mr. Davin.

Scattered applause.

Davin: My friends, the North-West is not tainted with the bigotry of Central Canada!

Moose Javian: Back to Ireland, you Papist! No surrender!

Davin: No surrender, the man croaks – and I repeat it. No surrender to the forces of darkness! We can *protect* French rights without becoming slaves of the Roman Church!

Moose Javian: Your own paper turned against you, traitor!

Davin: Who dares call Davin a traitor! It was Scott who betrayed me! We had an agreement! Well, I've fixed Mr. Scott! This afternoon, I filed a legal suit to protect my rights! As of tomorrow morning, Walter Scott will be barred from entering *The Regina Leader*.

Crowd: What? What's going on?

Saunders: Mr. Davin –

Davin: I am resuming control of my paper – and am appointing Mr. Endo Saunders as interim editor!

Saunders: Me? Oh, no! I couldn't – !

Burroughs: Accept with a show of gratitude, lad.

Moose Javian: Looks like a Catholic to me.

Davin: Mr. Saunders is a loyal man, which is more than I can say for some of the Conservatives in this city.

Scattered boos.

You think it's a vacation in Ottawa! Well, it isn't, it's damned hard work. Like a treadmill – I have no time for family, or my own life –

Moose Javian: Aaa – quit bellyachin', you damned Dogan!

Saunders: Quiet, you!

Davin slips and staggers to his seat.

Moose Javian: Look! He's drunk and maudlin! Davin's a drunken Dogan! *Takes up a chant.* Davin, the drunken Dogan! Davin, the drunken Dogan!

Saunders attacks him. Burroughs gets involved. Big uproar. Burroughs blows a police whistle. Silence.

Burroughs: All right – Mr. Davin has perhaps supped of the grape too freely this evening! What man doesn't? Does McInnis pretend to be a teetotaler? Mr. Davin has been under a lot of strain! He is a newly married man! *Some laughs.* And even tipsy, Davin is a better man than the Liberal McInnis!

Saunders: Hear, hear!

Moose Javian: Make him apologize! Apologize! Apologize!

Burroughs turns to Davin.

Davin: Gentlemen – your Member of Parl'men' stands censured – and repentant. Davin will take the pledge!

Crowd: *The Pledge*!

Davin takes out his flask, empties it on the ground.

Davin: Mr. Saunders! Write this down. It will appear in every newspaper in the territory – including McInnis' *Regina Standard* – if he dares accept it. "I, Nicholas Flood Davin, hereby renounce the use of alcohol, and resolve to become a strict abstainer! I will use all my influence in the cause of Christian temperance! Drinking has been the bane of my life and I vow to quit it forever! Signed, Nicholas Flood Davin."

Moose Javian: He's lying! He'll be plastered again tomorrow!

Burroughs: Enough! Now Mr. Davin's pledge on the eve of an election, may appear suspicious –

Moose Javian: Suspicious! *Laughs.*

Burroughs: But he has the courage to make it in public! And we challenge McInnis to do the same!

Applause and cheers for Davin. Lights fade.

SCENE THREE * * *

Lights go up on Leader *office. Saunders is setting large type on a "stick." Scott appears.*

Scott: Hello, Endo.

Saunders: *Startled.* What are you doing in here?

Scott: It is my newspaper tomorrow – one way or another – after the vote.

Saunders: I got one more edition still to run.

Scott: Nicholas here?

Saunders: Down at campaign headquarters. Shouldn't you be at the returning office? Counting ballots or something?

Scott: The returning officer merely oversees the process, Endo. We hire workers to do the tallies. They can reach me on the telephone.

Saunders: What, uh – how does it look?

Scott: McInnis has a lead in early returns. Almost 20 votes.

Saunders: We expected that.

Scott: McInnis predicts a 200-vote margin of victory.

Saunders: 'At's nothing. We predicted 500 for Davin. And we got the victory article set and ready to run. *Shows Scott.*

Scott: We'll let history be the judge. Davin's own flip-flopping has condemned him. The people are ready to break the Tory stranglehold. Eighteen years is a long time, Endo.

Saunders: Listen – go somewhere else, will you?

Davin enters behind them.

Scott: I'm not welcome?

Saunders: No – yer not!

Davin: Nonsense, Endo. Mr. Scott is welcome to stay as long as he likes – overnight, if need be. Tomorrow, it's all his.

Scott: I came to wish you luck.

Davin: Luck wins no elections, Walter. Hard work and a clear conscience do. If I lived by luck, I'd still be digging potatoes in Ballyscanlon. Do stay and join our celebration.

Scott: You're not bitter?

Davin: Nonsense. A lawsuit between friends is a good test of intellect. And you?

Scott: *Pause.* As you say, it's mine tomorrow, anyway. I am still grateful. *Pause.* You're managing without your flask?

Davin: *Grins.* It's amazing how that became McInnis' problem, isn't it?

Saunders: Article's written, Mr. Davin. *Indicates.* Just put the totals in those blanks.

Davin: *Reading*. Hm. "Demolished?" No. Make that "Slaughtered!"

Scott: Aren't you being a *bit* presumptuous?

Davin: Have you heard the tally? McInnis is only 12 votes up! We're going to beat the pants off him!

Scott: You've never trailed before, Nicholas. Doesn't that make you nervous?

Davin: Not a bit. Now we wait for the rural stations to report. The country vote goes to Davin.

Scott: In the past.

Music of a band is heard, off, playing "Hail the Conquering Hero" or some other triumphant march. Phone rings. Saunders answers.

Saunders: Results in from Qu'Appelle! Davin 37, McInnis 45.

Scott: You see?

Davin: Thanks Endo. Did you remember to vote?

Saunders: Yessir. First thing this morning.

Davin: And you doubt that Davin will sweep this election? There's over a dozen polls to be heard from – and he's only 20 votes up!

Saunders: It'll be hours before the others come in, Mr. Davin. Go home and get some rest.

Davin: Rest! On the night of my greatest election victory?

Scott: The rural polls won't be here until morning, Nicholas. Don't worry. I'll make sure the tally is honest.

The band is quite loud now, with sounds of shouting.

Davin: By God, it's the same tune! The night of Disraeli's election – the first I ever reported! That's what hooked me into politics! The drama of election night. There's only one night in politics, gentlemen – the night judgement is rendered.

Phone rings. Saunders answers.

Saunders: Results from Milestone! Davin 24, McInnis 19!

Davin: What did I tell you? Now the tide is turning!

Saunders: And Wood Mountain: Davin 31, McInnis 40.

Pause. Scott and Saunders exchange glances.

Scott: What is all that noise?

Saunders looks out.

Saunders: Liberals. Carryin' J.K. McInnis up and down Broad Street on their shoulders! A big gang of 'em. Headin' for their victory celebration.

Davin: *Laughs.* The fools! They've no idea!

Scott: McInnis is holding the lead. You have to consider the possibility of defeat.

Davin: Never! He doesn't stand a chance. He is only making himself ridiculous with this parade.

Saunders: I'm going down to the returning officer to check. Those tallies can't be right!

Saunders goes out. Music fades in distance.

Scott: *Awkwardly.* Mrs. Hayes said to say hello.

Davin: Please reciprocate. How is she?

Scott: Living creatively. She has a millinery shop.

Davin: She shouldn't have given up the library. Does she still – write?

Scott: Her first volume is coming out. Published in Winnipeg.

Davin: Ah. Please tender my congratulations.

Scott: Is, er, Mrs. Davin with you?

Davin: No. No. The train travel is too exhausting.

Scott gets up, fiddling with a stick of type.

Scott: This is ridiculous!

Davin: What is?

Scott: Waiting. For the sentence! Nicholas – don't you see? It's over! You're through!

Davin: Walter, I shall be sorry to disappoint you.

Scott: How can you live in such monumental self-delusion!

Davin: *Brightly.* Remember – "If the sun and moon should doubt – they'd immediately go out."

Scott: Damn you!

Scott hurls the tray of type at the floor.

Get out of my print-shop! Go and find your own hole to die in! I'm finished with you!

Davin attempts to speak, looks into Scott's eyes and defeat. He turns towards the exit.

No! No – wait.

Davin pauses.

Nicholas, I – I didn't mean that.

Davin: I know.

Scott: I'm sorry. Please. I'll wait with you – for the results. I, uh, will want to get a statement.

Davin: All right. I'll wait.

During the following scene, Davin circulates, picking up the pieces of type and placing them back in the stick.

Self-delusion, eh, Walter?

Scott: Yes.

Davin: You have matched me in journalism. And God knows, you may yet be a politician. But you're not one to live a life of fantasy. You'll never be a poet.

Scott: It was an ambition I gave up long ago.

Davin: Oh – it's not an ambition. It's a condition. And you can't give it up if you have it. It's a way of seeing – you know what I mean?

Scott: I'm afraid not.

Davin: You have to start as I did, in Kilfinane – an ironmonger's apprentice at the age of ten. By God, then you know the value of a gifted tongue! I picked that lesson up, the first time I ran off to Dublin. I learned enough in three days to know I'd never go back to the hardware trade. Or to the Catholic Church.

Scott: You? A *Catholic*?

Davin: Yes – and descended from O'Devin, King of Ulster in the 6th Century. The O'Devins stood against Cromwell in the defense of Clonmel. But I left that doomed heritage and made my way to London at the age of 19. Fame and fortune! Now those are *illusions*, my lad! Real illusions! Nothing is impossible to a boy who survived the famines of County Limerick! The Middle Temple? A cake-walk! Press Gallery of the British House of Commons. *That* was the rock from which men of *letters* were hewn. Coleridge. Dickens. Hazlitt.

Scott: It seems a long way away now.

Davin: I was at the centre of the universe, only 40 years ago. The politicians I knew! Disraeli, Bright. John Stuart Mill was there – looked like a simpleton! I covered the Franco-Prussian War for the *London Standard*. Have I told you?

Scott: No.

Davin: At the Battle of Gravelotte, I watched the French Infantry beat back a dozen cavalry charges – each one more magnificently disastrous than before. I walked over ground where dead men lay in stacks six feet deep. And while they died and rotted so gallantly, the French politicians and merchants made fortunes in profiteering. But I returned from that war, Mr. Scott, with my illusions intact. Believe it or not. I decided to turn to the new world, following the footsteps of Thomas D'Arcy McGee. Brief fling in law and politics, until I wore Toronto out – then the Old Man himself advised me to pursue my illusions in the North-West. I created a new reality, Walter, from my illusions. And it *exists*! Like that printing press! Real as iron – and full of illusions.

He set the stick of type down.

Scott: You have had a good life, Nicholas. A full and fortunate one. But the time ultimately comes –

Saunders runs in, gasping.

Saunders: All the polls but one! McInnis – declared – the winner!

Scott: How many?

Saunders: Twenty votes. Shows a paper. Gave me his – victory statement – to run in *The Leader*.

Davin: I'll take that.

Davin takes it and rips it in four, drops it on the floor.

J.K. McInnis should have more respect for the electoral process. There is still one more poll.

Scott: That does it! *Tries to pick up the shreds.* You can be as arrogant as you like – but I have to live in this town! For me, there *is* a tomorrow!

Phone rings. Scott answers.

Scott: Votes are in from Dundurn!

Saunders: And?

Scott: He swept the poll! *To Davin.* Twenty-four to four! *It's a tie vote.*

Saunders: What?

Scott: I can't believe it!

Davin: No sense of illusion, Walter?

Saunders: So who wins?

Davin: By law the returning officer must cast the tie-breaking vote. Walter?

Scott: Me?

Davin: Execute your duty – without favouritism or prejudice.

Saunders: Well?

Scott: I vote – Davin.

Explosion of applause.

Davin: I was wrong, Walter. You *do* have the makings of a poet. See? Imagination!

Saunders: They'll be roaring their heads off at headquarters, Mister Davin. Let's go!

Saunders and Davin depart. The band music starts up again. Scott picks up the stick of type, looks, grins.

Scott: "Davin Wins Again!"

Music: "Wild Colonial Boy." Lights fade. Sound of train builds.

Scene Four * * * *

Burroughs enters the House of Commons, joined by Davin.

Burroughs: Well, Nicholas. It will feel strange in Opposition.

Davin: It's the same game, Stanley. Just the downturn of the wheel.

Burroughs: Well – Laurier gets the credit. He killed us on the Manitoba Schools issue. You're our only member from the North-West.

Davin: The Party will take a generation to recover – if ever.

Burroughs: Still – you did all right, eh Nicholas? One vote! The Honourable Member from Walter Scott!

They laugh.

Davin: As the gallant Mercutio said of his wound: "Tis not so deep as a well, nor so wide as a church-door, but tis enough."

Both: "T'will serve!"

They take their seats. Horsnall appears opposite, smirking.

Davin: Mr. Speaker, studying Mr. Laurier and his cohorts from this new perspective, I see a wondrous beast indeed. I am reminded of Virgil's description of Scylla:

> At top it shows a gracious face
> The breast replete with human grace.
> The rest is all an ugly whale
> With maw of wolf and fish's tail!

We have the gracious talk of the Prime Minister, but the maw of the wolf is seen on the faces of his ministers! *Horsnall scowls.* The rest beggar imagination – but they smell of fish. Their unredeemed pledges are so numerous the government looks like an overstuffed pawnshop!

Horsnall: Objection!

Davin: They come not to speak, but to listen to their leader speak, and leap about like harlequins! The leader plays Faust to Clifford Sifton, the Mephistopheles of the Interior. As for that man Horsnall – !

Horsnall: On a point of privilege, Mr. Speaker! The member must not say "that man," but use the parliamentary mode of address!

Davin: Did I say "that man," Mr. Speaker? I apologize to the Honourable Member. I am sorry I called him a man – and I retract my thoughtless remark.

Laughter. Desk thumping. Burroughs pulls Davin to his seat. Lights fade. Music: "Dromore."

SCENE FIVE * * * * *

Lights up on Leader *office. 1899. Saunders is dummying a page. He now wears glasses. Davin enters diffidently.*

Saunders: Mr. Davin! Long time no see!

Davin: Hello, Endo. You know how it is – *waves vaguely* – Ottawa.

Saunders: Yes, I know. You're doing well?

Davin: *With forced heartiness.* I made a great speech in Boston! I expect *The Leader* carried it?

Saunders: I, uh, don't recall.

Davin: I represented the Dominion there during the Queen's Jubilee. Spoke on "The Empire."

> There is no clime so hospitable,
> no tract so dangerous, no sea so lone,
> but over tower and turret and dome,
> over scud and sand and palmtree –

Saunders: No – I don't recall it.

Davin: Oh well. How runs *The Leader*?

Saunders: Not bad. Mr. Scott promoted me to managing editor.

Davin: You always had the makings of a good newspaperman.

Saunders: What brings you to town, Mr. Davin?

Davin: You haven't heard? I am establishing a new newspaper! *The Regina West*!

Saunders: *Shocked.* Really?

Davin: Yes – in fact I'm looking for an editor. I could use a man with your experience.

Saunders: *Uncomfortable.* A new paper, eh? Conservative?

Davin: Of course. I have Sir Charles Tupper's backing. And Dewdney's. The Territories need a strong voice against Laurier.

Saunders: Gee – he's awful popular these days!

Davin: Only because they're promoting massive immigration out here. Sifton stole that plan from me.

Saunders: You, uh, capitalizing this newspaper yourself, Mr. Davin?

Davin: Well – my wife has a sizeable investment. Sound businesswoman, my Eliza. You've never met her, Endo?

Saunders: No sir. Don't believe she ever came West.

Davin: Oh, it's an exhausting train trip. But we're moving out here now! Buying a house on Lorne Street.

Saunders: You plan to stay then?

Davin: This is my home, Endo! I must be here, with my constituents! Tough election battle coming up!

Saunders: *Cautiously.* I expect so. You running again, Mr. Davin?

Davin: I haven't, er, decided yet. I hear rumours that Walter is going for the Liberal nomination – is that true?

Saunders: Aw, you'd have to talk to him, Mr. Davin.

Davin: He's, um, not here today?

Saunders: Um – no. Not this afternoon.

Davin: Where would I find him?

Saunders: At Mrs. Hayes', sir. I believe there's a party – to celebrate her, uh, birthday.

Strains of music in the background, tinkling of glasses, etc.

Davin: Kate's – birthday?

Saunders: I'm sure – if she knew you were here, she'd have invited you.

Davin: *Lost.* My God – her birthday. August already?

Saunders: It's actually a farewell. She's moving to Winnipeg – to work for *The Free Press.*

Davin: What? *Free Press?*

Saunders: Yes sir. First lady journalist in the West!

Davin: *Laughs at a memory.* Ah – Kate! It was I, you know, who first discerned her golden talent. I coached her first efforts.

Saunders: Yes, I remember.

Davin: And to think she was published in London. In London! A great honour, Endo!

Saunders: You're dead right there, sir. Now, if you'll excuse me – I have to get this page to the compositors –

Davin: Of course, of course! One other thing, Endo. The, uh, new campaign will be starting shortly and I – that is, I need a campaign manager and I thought if you were – free –

Saunders: I wish I could help, Mr. Davin – but I've, uh, joined the Liberals.

Davin: Oh. *Joking.* Well, you wouldn't be much help, would you?

Saunders: No sir – guess not. *Moves toward the door.*

Davin: The Liberals are clever to recruit in the West. That's Sifton's influence!

Saunders: Good night, Mr. Davin.

Scene Six * * * * * *

Lights up on Kate and Scott, after the party, laughing. Davin appears at the door.

Kate: Nicholas!

Scott: Good Lord!

Nicholas: Hello –

Kate: Why didn't you come sooner? You've just missed Enid Bartlett!

Davin: Oh – well – I – political business, you know.

Kate: I'll heat up the tea!

Davin: Hm? Oh – no, thanks – I just – dropped by.

Kate: A glass of sherry then. Have you heard? I'm leaving for Winnipeg in a few days.

Davin: Winnipeg?

Kate: A lovely city – so cosmopolitan.

Davin: And the children?

Kate: Elaine will pursue her singing career at last. They're at the park this afternoon – but you could see them tomorrow, if you're in town.

Davin: They're – fine children.

Kate: Well, Nicholas – it's never too late! We could still see a junior Davin haranguing the citizens some day.

Pause.

Scott: How is Mrs. Davin?

Davin: Hm? Oh, well, thank you. We are moving here.

Kate: To Regina?

Davin: Yes. Forced to really. The election, you know.

Kate: What a pity. I'll regret not meeting your wife. *Pause.* A lot of water has passed below the bridge, Nicholas.

Davin: Yes – yes indeed.

Scott: I expect you heard I am being offered the Liberal nomination.

Davin: I did hear that.

Scott: I, uh, don't know what your plans are –

Davin: I will run for the Conservatives, of course.

Scott: I see.

Kate: What Walter is trying to say, Nicholas – is that he feels badly about running against you.

Davin: Well, you'll be sorry, my boy. The voters will demand a seat for me in the cabinet this time. And once I reach cabinet – anything is possible.

Kate: There are so many alternatives, Nicholas – you have great poems to write! And plays! Your memoirs!

Davin: Yes. Yes indeed. Well, I must see to my constituents. Good-bye. Kate – if you need help –

Kate: Help? Why would I need help?

Davin: Well – with the children.

Kate: No, no they're independent now!

Davin goes out.

Kate: How odd. Do you suppose he – ?

Scott: No. He doesn't know. Couldn't know.

Lights fade.

Scene Seven * * * * * * *

A political rally. Moose Javian enters, then Saunders. Scott and Davin enter. Scott leaps on to the platform with agility. Davin slips and nearly falls trying to imitate him.

Saunders: Ladies and gentlemen, the candidates have agreed to speak in a series of public debates, with a two-minute time limit. Mr. Davin won the toss, and will speak first.

Davin: Thank you, Endo. I did offer to speak last – but wisdom precedes innocence. Hahaha! *He laughs alone.* But seriously, ladies and gentlemen – and I must speak to you seriously, for we only have a moment – this election is absolutely critical. We are on the threshold of the Twentieth Century! And to ride the crest of this great wave, we need a man who represents the future! Now Mr. Scott is a reasonable man – a good man, but he is a candidate of the corrupt Sifton machine! He represents a clique of Eastern monopolies, a Siftonite – a lackey of the man responsible for flooding our the territory with foreign immigrants!

Moose Javian: Aaaa – yer a damn foreigner yerself!

Davin: *Rattled.* What?

Moose Javian: Who let you outtuv Ireland, Davin?

Davin: *Ignoring him.* Furthermore, this Judas has stooped to using *The Regina Leader* – a once proud and independent journal – to slander me and the Conservative Party. It would not suprise me if the Liberals had organized a gang of thugs to intimidate honest electors – !

Saunders: *Looking at watch.* Ten seconds.

Davin: What? Ten – ? *Quickly.* I stood up to the Grits in '96! Now Sifton's minions are out to make sure I don't succeed again. They have even forced Commissioner Herchmer of the Mounted Police into retirement – an old Tory supporter – and appointed a Grit. Scott sits there looking innocent, but his hands are stained with the same blood– !

Saunders: *Forced to interrupt.* Time, Mr. Davin. Thank you.

Saunders and Scott lead the light applause.

Scott: Thank you. Ladies and gentlemen. *Pause.* Mr. Davin has said a number of things, some of which deserve rebuttal, and others which we may let pass by. As far as *The Leader* goes, I can only say that reporting Mr. Davin's speeches has not been easy, as they have been torrents of personal abuse couched in the foulest Billingsgate. Where are the issues? Are we to report only the fierce screech of a defeated man? *Pause.* Mr. Davin has served this community for a number of years. But the territory has grown up. He was a worthy representative in the Age of Confederation, but we are entering the Age of Prosperity. I invite you to support the party of Prosperity and Commerce. Frankly, I think Mr. Davin should have had the sense to retire gracefully, and not end his career in such an undignified manner –

Davin: *Outraged.* Retire! I'll retire you, ye bloody git!

Saunders: Thank you, gentlemen. The next debate will be at 8 p.m. tomorrow in the ballroom of the Clayton Hotel. Remember to cast your ballot on November 7th!

Light fades.

Scene Eight * * * * * * * *

Davin enters Leader *office.*

Davin: Oh – Endo.

Saunders: Hi, Mr. Davin – paper?

Davin: Those ballots were blatantly forged!

Saunders: I'm sorry Mr. Davin. People here just ain't grateful, I giss.

Davin: A politician who looks for gratitude is a fool. You know what Cromwell said, when the mobs cheered him into Parliament! "They'd cheer the same if I were being led to the chopping block!"

Saunders: So, yuh going to this reception for the Duke and Duchess of York?

Davin: Hm?

Saunders: They'll be in town next week.

Davin: No, I don't think so.

Saunders: Really! Every big cheese in town is going!

Davin: I was, uh, not invited. Limited, er, space on the platform.

Saunders: Isn't that a corker?

Davin: Mrs. Davin was invited, as president of the Daughters of the Empire. She felt I had been snubbed, however – and declined the invitation.

Saunders: So, I giss yer kind of at loose ends?

Davin: Oh no. Not at all. I'm going to Winnipeg next week. Premier Roblin of Manitoba has offered me a position. My talents can be put to use.

Saunders: Well, good luck. S'pose you'll be looking up Mrs. Hayes?

Davin: I – what – ?

Saunders: Kate. She'd be real glad to see you.

Davin: Oh – I couldn't, Endo! I am a married man!

Lights fade as Davin goes off. Sound of locomotive bridges to next scene.

SCENE NINE * * * * * * * * *

Lights up on a neutral area. Davin approaches

Secretary: *Off.* Sorry, I don't see your name here. Devlin, you said?

Davin shakes his head, raises his hand.

Well, as you can see, there is no Davin, nor any MP expected by Mr. Roblin. *Pause.* Sorry.

Davin turns, shaking his head. He shuffles to another corner of the stage.

Kate: *Off.* Child, Nicholas? What child? You must be mistaken. How did you come by this notion?

Light goes up in a third corner. Davin shuffles toward it, removing a revolver from his pocket.

Salesman: *Off.* You can't fire it? You wanted this fer cats, didden yuh, sir? Okay, look – getcher hand outta the way. Ya hafta cock the hammer – like so. Got it?

Davin puts the gun back in his pocket, crosses stage.

Bellboy: *Off.* Letter for Mr. Davin! Is Mr. Davin in the hotel?

Davin takes the letter.

It's from Regina, sir. From a – Mrs. Davin? No reply?

Davin puts it unopened into his jacket pocket and goes off.

Voice: Mr. Davin?

Knocking on door.

You wanted a call 30 minutes before train time! Regina train leaves in a few minutes. Mr. Davin?

Knocking is repeated.

Conductor: *Off.* Now boarding on Platform One. All aboard for Portage, Brandon, Regina, and points West!

Sound of train chugging out of the station.

All aboarrrrrrd!

Epilogue

A small light on the old woman.

Old Woman: My father's life was a story of trains. Trains caught and – trains missed. I took a few myself, collecting pieces of his story. Our story. I learned why I grew up in a convent orphanage. My only visitor was my Aunt Kate – who told me on my twelfth birthday I was her daughter. And I learned nothing about him. Until years later – when it was too late. If he had only known about me – he could have come to me in Winnipeg – a few blocks away – after he missed the train. But he stayed alone in his room with the gun and – a few seconds later – don't be alarmed now –

Revolver fired, off.

Old Woman: – my father's story ended. Except for me, of course. And the trains. . . .

Distant whistle of locomotive. Lights out.

The End

Gone the Burning Sun

Playwright's Introduction: Bethune

My relations with Henry Norman Bethune go back long before I read Ted Allan's and Sydney Gordon's biography, *The Scalpel and The Sword*,[1] though I was unaware of any connection at the time. I was fascinated by their gripping account of this iconoclast who became an icon – long before I discovered he was a distant cousin.

I made this discovery in 1980 while doing genealogical research in Scotland. My great-great-great-grandmother was a Beaton from the Isle of Mull. In fact, she was one of a legendary tribe of Seven Beaton Sisters.[2] When I went out to the Hebrides to explore Mull, I learned that the Beatons and the Bethunes were one and the same family. It was an electrifying experience. When I reached the furthest point in the journey at the western tip of the Ross of Mull, and set foot on the Sacred Isle of Iona, I could feel the drama taking shape. There I learned that the Beatons and Bethunes (and Betons and Beatouns) were descendents of medieval forebears who travelled to Iona from Bethune, in northern France. They were monks and herbalists who followed St. Columba to one of the earliest missions of Christianity, founded in 863 at Iona, a sacred site of the ancient Druids and burial ground of the great Scottish kings, including Duncan and Macbeth.

The Scottish Historical Records office in Edinburgh became my second home that year (I was a Scottish-Canadian Exchange Writer in 1979-80). My third home became the University of Edinburgh's Department of Chinese Studies just off George Square.

The following year I obtained a teaching appointment at Nanjing University in Southern China – and took my family along with me on the adventure of a lifetime, following Norman Bethune's career around China. My hosts also sent me along on a couple of other noteworthy treks (parts of Mao Zedong's Long March of 1934-35, and its even more remarkable predecessor – the Taiping Army's advance on Nanjing in 1852).

On the streets of Nanjing and in the surrounding countryside, I discovered a lot about Norman Bethune. The "people's love" for Bethune is not political hype. There are books, films, postage stamps, paper-cuts, even comic books idealizing Norman Bethune, emblazoned with his heroic profile. Everybody over thirty in China can recite from memory Mao's essay "In Praise of Norman Bethune" written upon his death.[3]

And everyone thought I was he, or at least a relative, and certainly a Canadian. There is a slight physical resemblance, though I believe I look more like V.I. Lenin. (In Chinese popular art, Bethune's image is significantly "Leninized.") Working people would see me on the street and yell out, "It's Dr. Bethune!"

That's when I knew I would write a one-man play about Dr. Norman Bethune. I thought of it as an artistic *passeport* to perform around China. At that point I put all research aside, and in the course of a two-week train journey through southern China, wrote the first draft of the play. Back in Canada, I rewrote it two or three times for workshops in Montreal and Regina, and in 1983, took it back to China, where I toured as an itinerant performer, soliciting criticism from Chinese audiences at universities and language schools. (The ill-fated movie *Bethune: The Making of a Hero* would have benefited from a similar "workshop.")

By then, the play was in development under the direction of Brian Richmond at Magnus Theatre. One-person shows had come of age in Canadian theatre, for obvious economic reasons, and were attracting an audience – as seen by the success of plays like *La Sagouine*, *Billy Bishop Goes to War*, *Maggie & Pierre*.

But we felt something more was needed, aside from a great biographical subject.

It came from China, naturally. For the music, we turned to another friend, David Liang, who had composed the score for *The Great Cultural Revolution*. Our hope was to create a portable, trans-Pacific theatre piece, a drama rather than a monologue, which would invoke the *Tao*, the Oriental "unity of opposites." Chinese music, English language; Chinese *pipa* player, Canadian actor; female, male; emotion and intellect. Such polar dualities are the only way to understand Norman Bethune, who was not only a bundle of contradictions but carried the burden of his own historical dialectics: Christian and Communist; medicine and politics; self-destructive but imbued with the life-force.

David Liang's music was a perfect Yin to the play's Yang, and our Taoist construction has prospered ever since. The 1984 première was at the Guelph Spring Festival, performed by David Fox and Pan Hui-zhu. The same performers took it on a tour of China in 1987, followed by a Canadian tour. The same season, it premièred in Melbourne, Australia, in a memorable production starring Rod Williams, and has since been performed throughout Canada by actors such as Duncan Fraser, Wayne Nicklaus and Ken Kramer. In 1989, I finally got to perform the play professionally myself on a tour of the Yukon and northern BC. This spring, I took it to Scotland, Germany, and Ireland. Norman Bethune's "spirit of internationalism" may have greater application than even Mao Zedong could prophesy.

What was this "spirit of internationalism?" What made Bethune a secular saint in China – so revered that his legend has outlasted even Mao? There were many more important figures in the Chinese revolution, including other Western physicians like Dr. George Hatem. But they lacked his inner conflicts, the roots of dramatic heroism.

What distinguished Bethune was less his Communist doctrine than his deep Christian humanism, which revealed itself in China.

Bethune was a marginal Communist – he had been virtually expelled in Spain – but he was steeped in the tradition of missionary service, from his youthful teaching stints at Frontier College to his stretcher-bearing during World War One. He had a Communist intellect, but a Christian soul – as one might expect with devout Presbyterian parents like the Rev. Malcolm Bethune and Elizabeth Goodwin.

Bethune, remember, was born in a manse. Norman's great-great-grandfather established the Church of Scotland in Canada, and became Upper Canada's first – in 1787 – Presbyterian minister. This was the Reverend John Bethune, the original immigrant from the Hebrides. Five of his six sons turned Anglican, and one became the Bishop of Toronto, another the Principal of McGill University. The sixth, Angus, turned his back on the establishment, became a fur trader, and eventually a Chief Factor of the Hudson's Bay. His son – Norman Senior, Bethune's grandfather – founded the medical faculty at Trinity College, University of Toronto. In 1859 while studying in Europe he volunteered his medical skills following the infamous Battle of Solferino, tending the wounded with Jean Dunant, the founder (three years later) of the International Red Cross.

But the Bethunes of Iona and the Hebrides had a heritage of Christian healing going back ten centuries. Bethune may have been conscious of this when he wrote in a 1935 letter, "You must remember my father was an evangelist and I come of a race of men violent, unstable, of passionate convictions and wrong-headedness, intolerant yet with it all a vision of truth and a drive to carry them on to it even though it leads, as it has done in my family, to their destruction." A questing but self-destructive rebel all his life, Norman could not disobey the commands of his own blood. And blood – with all its complex symbolism – dominates *Gone the Burning Sun*.

Norman was a complex man – unconventional, a brilliant writer, egocentric and arrogant. Even the Chinese didn't understand him that well. Yet in China Bethune somehow redeemed himself. China gave meaning to his life – his last chance to prove he was more than a dilettante adventurer. Facing destiny, he supressed his inner demons and became the exemplar of "the internationalist spirit" – a modern archetype of the humanist physician.

He did this by becoming a martyr – the most elevated form of self-destruction, more profound than anything he'd attempted in Canada, the US and Spain. He sacrificed himself for the people of China and – to my thinking – did it quite consciously. Within a year of his death in the Wutai Mountains in 1939, Bethune transcended mere historical recognition to attain the realm of mythology. He was rediscovered by Canadians in the idealistic 1960s, and lionized in the pragmatic 1970s when the government began opening trade and communications links to China.

Bethune's uncanny ability to locate himself at the centre of the century's major social struggles made him an "internationalist." His intimate relationship with these historical forces made him a hero – and the ideal subject for biographical drama.

---

1. Ted Allen and Sydney Gordon, *The Scalpel and the Sword*, revised, Monthly Review Press: New York, 1973.
2. E. Jennings, *Seven Beaton Sisters: A Family Tree*, Toronto, 1941.
3. *Mao Ze Dong*, Foreign Languages Press: Beijing, 1967.

David Fox as Dr. Norman Bethune, Guelph Spring Festival, Guelph, 1984.

First Performance

Gone The Burning Sun was first performed at the Guelph Spring Festival in May 1984, in a co-production with Magnus Theatre of Thunder Bay. The play then moved to Magnus Theatre for a further run. Directed by Brian Richmond with music by David Liang, in both productions the cast was as follows:

Dr. Norman Bethune - *David Fox*
Musician – *Pan Hui-zhu*

Gone the Burning Sun

Scene One

There is a minimal set: table, chair, perhaps a coat rack with clothing.

Music. Lights come up on Norman Bethune, lying on a table apparently dead. He is coming out of anaesthetic.

Bethune: Frances . . . Frances . . . *Moves.* Hmm? Where am I? Oh . . . ward. Right – operation. Right. *He sits up suddenly, calls.*

Frances, where are you!? *Looks around.*

Oh, Barney. Am I back? For a minute, I thought I was – you know – dead . . . . Did I make it?

He tries painfully to rise from the bed.

By God, I'm alive. Barney, I'm alive! I slid past the big knife! That means you'll do it, too. And we're going to march out of this mausoleum together! Nurse, give me a hand! Yes – now! Oh!

He crosses to the chair. He sits, and slowly begins to dress.

Whew! Back from the dead. Powerful – that anaesthetic. Dreams. I was in a very strange place – heaven, I suppose. Buncha people standing around gawking at me. Very odd, Barney – here's the thing – they were all – oriental! Do you think God's angels might be Chinese? *Laughs.* No. Frances was there too. . . .

He looks around.

Come on, I have to get out of this abattoir before the rot sets in again! I can't believe it, Barney – I'm actually alive! Radical pneumothorax – and I made it! So much for Doctor Warren's "rest cures" and all that mumbo-jumbo! So y'see – there is hope. You are going to do it too, old buddy!

Dangerous? Yeah, I guess. They cut away half of my rib cage! But what did I have to lose? No hope. Separated from Frances. Broke as a tramp. A hundred bucks a day just to *stay* in this sanitorium. More like a luxury hotel, for cripe's sake. All my equipment in hock. And bills at home piling up like a January snowbank.

Impatient? Christ, if I wasn't so patient, I'd have slashed my throat weeks ago!

Know what I told Warren? "Doc, you're talking pure bullshit! This elegant Yankee rest home is *not* the way to treat critical TB. Don't you even read the damn medical literature? Take a bloody chance!" That's when he hands me that "excessive risk" crapola! I tell ya, Barney, not one of these idiots know what's being done in their own field! They're gonna force me to take up lung surgery! "Doc," I says, "This patient needs a new prognosis. If Bethune doesn't get his nicotine and whiskey, he's gonna *die*. I want to walk out of this morgue! I got a marriage to put back together! Listen, if *I'm* willing to take the goddamn risk – why can't you? I spent a year bearing stretchers in the stinking slaughter-grounds of Flanders – I *earned* the right to take a chance. Sure – collect all the opinions you want, but I warn you, Doc – if you don't cut into me and collapse the bad lung – I swear, I'll do it myself!"

He lights a cigarette.

So they operated. And I survived! Barney, for the first time in months, I believe I might make it! Nothing less than a resurrection – that's what you're seeing!

He sings and dances.

"Farewell ye dungeons dark and strong
Farewell, farewell to thee."
He sang his tune as he danced around
Below the gallows tree.

A great day in medical history! April 25, 1927. A TB patient prescribes his own surgery and lives to tell the tale!

He takes a deep drag on the cigarette, coughs.

Hey! Feeling strong enough to sneak into town and hit the bootleggers for a bottle of whiskey? That's my man! To hell with the rules! Oh don't worry, I'll take it easy. I should send a note to Frances! No – I haven't told her about the operation. She ran back to Edinburgh to be with her daddy – simply couldn't manage the slums of Detroit. Well, I can't blame her. Not when I left her to fight off the creditors all by herself. *Calls.* Barney! Make that two bottles!

He sits to write on a sheet of paper.

My darling Frances. I hasten to fill my long absence – *Crosses out.* – I am now in a position to clarify – *Crosses out.* – I miss you, Fannie.

He addresses her directly, smiles.

"Frightfully." And I frighten you miserably, I know I do. So I understand why you abandoned me to the fleshpots of a Yankee Sanitorium! Unfortunately, the expense here is exorbitant. If you were able to sell off our furniture, perhaps you could advance me a small portion? A temporary loan. I offer a wistful promise to restore your bank account when I am fully recovered. This may be soon! To the dismay of my doctor, I remain on this side of death's door.

Look. We need to make a new beginning. Back in Canada. Maybe Montreal! Oh, you'd love Montreal! The world will be our garden again – if we can only learn to value what we know, and understand what we don't. Like why my Canuck craziness needs your kind of Scottish stability. Or why I can't keep a professional distance from my patients, in the way you want. I'm just a lumberjack, Frannie. I know I bruise your sensibility. I've never associated with the right sort of women – and that's why you hypnotized me so completely. Will it help with your folks if you explained that? I doubt it. But we have to keep going – even through the fights – which have nothing to do with money, not really – there's something else – that lies at the very centre.

He shakes his head, returns to writing.

I think about you now, remembering your – glowing eyes, your radiant flesh. It makes me well again. Your "kent-speckle" Canadian – Beth.

He signs the letter, seals it into an envelope.

Sealed With A Kiss.

He paces around, studying his mural.

God – Barney's right. These murals are morbid. Doom-laden and decadent. "The TB's Progress!" Not the old Bethune spirit at all. Well, what do you expect from a man on deathrow? Little rays of sunshine bursting out of the heavens?

Nine panels. A journey through the valley of death. Five more, and I could do the stations of the cross! An epic drama in one act – "Bethune Pursued by the Tubercle Bacillus!"

He stops at the first panel, strikes a pose.

First station: "Youth At the Helm." Straight out of Gravenhurst, our hero surveys the world, opening before him like a flower. Note the glow of confidence on his face! Next: "The Castle of Heart's Desire," haunted by the Seven Sirens. Fame. Success. Wealth, Oh, what seductive songs they sing. But just as he approaches the castle – the TB monster plummets to the attack! Bethune falls to the River of Blood. Was the Castle of Heart's Desire a cruel delusion? Oh but – wait, what's this? – another castle – Trudeau Sanitorium. Will the hero live or die? Is there hope for survival after all? Yes!

I just have to erase this last gloomy panel. My Angel of Death. *Reads the inscription.*

Sweet Death, thou kindest angel of all,
In thy soft arms at last, O let me fall.
Bright stars are out, long gone the burning sun.
My little act is over, the tiresome play is done.

Norman Bethune. 1890-1927.

Cradled in those dark arms –

No! You black bitch – I won't erase you yet. I'm going to leave you behind – a joke for my dying friends. *Someone* has escaped your clutches – eh, sweetheart?

He chucks her under the chin.

Hey! Back with the booze, Barney! Hm? A letter? From Detroit! Frannie?

He picks up the envelope, opens it.

From her lawyer. *Reacts.* A divorce! *Crumples it.* That blood-sucker! A divorce! How *could* she? Just when I – *Turns in a fury.* Her family put her up to this! I'll go over there – plant a case of dynamite – blow up their "Great King Street" smugness! Stubborn bloody Scots – bitch! Well, they'll be damned lucky! *Picks the letter up again.* "Seeking fifteen hundred in cash and twenty-five thousand more in monthly installments!" Ha! You can't squeeze blood from a turnip, boys! *Throws it away.* I'm so deep in debt – my patients charge *me* interest.

Barney, old pal – I'm going to throw a party for my fellow zombies! Right here in the ward! Invite everybody who can still crawl! And the nurses! Hey, how about the girl from Texas – the one with the green eyes and the uh – overdeveloped thorax? *Laugh.* I thought that'd bring a light to your eye! It's time for the biggest, raunchiest, drunkenest bacchanal these greenish walls have ever frowned upon. We are going to make death *rumba*!

Scene Two

Bethune is sitting on the table. He is swinging his legs, wearing a white hospital coat.

Bethune: Good morning, gentlemen! Welcome to the Montreal Royal Victoria Hospital, jewel in the crown of international medico-pulmonary surgery. Now – what does that mean to innocent young interns like yourselves? *Pause, laughs.*

You're absolutely right, son – sweet bugger-all! Because it's no better than some waterfront abortion den when you look at the statistics. Riddled with bureaucracy and rotten with incompetence. So don't look for a medical utopia – here or anywhere else. The inefficiency will make you sweat. The hypocrisy will make you puke. More patients die in the Royal Vic from the cautious fumbling of old men than they do from TB in the slums of Verdun. *Pause.*

Cynical? Not at all. Realistic. To expect better would only create disillusionment. And God knows, there are enough disillusioned doctors already.

Four years ago, *I* was given a second life – through radical pneumothorax – so I left general practice and became a lung surgeon. One of the best. There are people here who accuse Bethune of *killing* his patients. Well, it's true. I do have a high mortality record. But the fact is, I operate on cases they're all terrified to admit into their offices – the hopeless dying! *Rises angrily.* So to hell with them! If you want to be lung surgeons, you'll follow *my* technique – fast diagnosis – out *there*, in the reeking streets of Montreal – fast operation, fast treatment! Yes they die on my operating table. But rememember, Bethune gives them a sporting chance!

He pulls a stethoscope from his pocket.

First demonstration this morning. Identify this instrument. *Points.* Right! I believe you have a future in medicine, son. Well, take a good look at the "stethoscope." The symbol of life – right? Wrong! This little device has killed more lung patients than all the cigarettes manufactured by Imperial Tobacco! My advice – wear it around your neck like a magic amulet. A bit of voodoo never hurt anyone. Remember – the doctor is the high priest. But for *results* – stick to your X-ray machine. Five hundred percent more reliable. And when you're ready to work – these!

He presents a set of heavy rib shears, gleaming.

Bethune Rib Shears. Look dangerous, don't they? Well, they're not made for delicacy. They're made to cut through a rib bone in one stroke – to collapse the lung – give it rest. TB is an extreme disease, gentlemen – and it demands extreme remedies. Make no mistake. You will get blood on your hands. And other unpleasant organisms. You'll have to overcome some pet aversions, see them for what they are.

Maggots, for example. Last month, I introduced forty-six live fly maggots into the chest cavity of one of my patients. Couldn't get the septic fluids to drain. Now maggots *love* to eat rotting flesh – and would you believe it? – within five days my little maggots had made him healthy – by consuming the entire infection. The despised vermin of this world can be valuable, gentlemen, if you allow yourselves to think in extremes.

A bell rings. He rushes off.

Consider these thoughts as you memorize your Latin. Tomorrow's lecture: "Bedside Manners and Bigger Fees!"

Scene Three

Bethune is at a table, writing.

Bethune: My darling Frances.

The winter snows of Montreal have descended. I dream that you are here, your tam glowing bright red up on the Mountain. And –

Edinburgh is a braw wee toon, but very grey in December. Dark. Like our outlaw courtship in George Square. *You* so Scottish, your wee bonny this, your wee thistle that – your stubbornness. And even then I could out-Scot you a hundredfold, and not just with the malt. Beaton – that was our family name – till my great-great-grand-daddy fled from the auld sod, and arrived in Montreal a Bethune.

Sings.

Yestre'en the Queen had four Marys,
This nicht she'll hae but three.
There's Mary Seaton and Mary Beaton
And Mary Carmichael and – me.

I do enjoy my work at the Royal Vic. If I thought I could make you happy as well, I'd declare "Come back and marry me again!" If we love each other, and it's obvious we do, why are we separated? Or – is it the *intensity* of my feeling that causes the problem? Perhaps if I didn't want you *all* the time – dreaming of caressing your smooth flesh – stimulating you to erotic acts – that shock you, I know – perhaps disgust you – then I wouldn't desire you at all. Can't love be spiritual and physical at the same time? I know I can learn to keep my carnal desires in check – if only you'll come back. There! I said it. Perhaps, if you did – we could meet as old friends. Live apart. But we'll rendez-vous on weekends for dinner and conversation, for drives in the country.

I miss you, Frannie. I want you here. But I know I mustn't dominate, or try to change you. Promise me you will consider it. Come and be thyself. The Frannie I knew in Edinburgh – self-contained and undistorted. Not some impossible fantasy of my youth. You see? I've matured.

Oh, Montreal is a world apart from Detroit. Very gentle, very quiet, very French. *Les allouettes* are fighting in the street for crumbs. And I identify with them. Looking for direction. I've started a children's art school with a couple of painter friends. Special project for slum kids. No fees, no cost. Work in my apartment. On Saturdays, I'll take my children to the art galleries, the children we'll never have. I wish you were here. God bless you.

He signs the letter.

Beth.

Scene Four

Bethune is jauntily dressed, with a bright scarf. He has a suitcase.

Bethune: Barney? You home? Barnwell, you old zombie!

Ahh! Might've known you'd emerge from this elegant woodwork somewhere! No, no special reason. Drove all the way to Michigan just to bend a friend's ear. Yeah. I depend on you to laugh at my jokes, Barney – Hell, you're the only one who even listens to me. Got any whiskey?

He removes the scarf, takes a glass.

Oh – you heard. Yes, Frannie and I married again. November. Wonderful ceremony. Only two years after the divorce. Romantic, eh? Frances *loved* it – far more sentimental than I. Cheers. Hmm? Oh – no, it's bust again, I'm sad to say. No, the same old story. Can't reconcile our irreconcilable natures. We get along beautifully – as long as we're not together. Oh, she's taking it all "splendidly." Now she's off to the kirk again – to marry our best man. Coleman – an old pal of mine, I think you met in Montreal. I'm sure they'll be very happy. No, no – we're all great friends. Barney, don't try to understand me. You never did before – and you always understood perfectly.

Well – yes. Fit as a fiddle, I suppose. Thirty miles on skis, every weekend. I know the Laurentians better than my own bronchial tubes. Regular workouts in the gym. I even do my own artificial pneumothorax now. You heard about my new machine? My latest invention!

He removes a machine from his suitcase and places it on the table. He removes his jacket and shirt.

With this little gadget, I keep my patients alive without the trauma of lung surgery. And all it really is, is an air pump. We just push the needle between the sixth and seventh ribs. Force air into the thoracic cavity. Bingo, lung is collapsed.

Here, I'll show you. No, I do it all the time. Can't trust my homicidal colleagues! Well – according to the gout-gang at the Royal Vic, this is dangerous lunacy. Self-treatment. Aaah, I don't fit in there, Barney. I think my career in lung surgery may be coming to an end.

He takes a large hypodermic needle.

Novocaine? Naah – don't believe in that stuff.

He plunges the needle into his chest.

There – just below the sixth rib. Now pump the air – into the chest – around the lung.

He coughs painfully, jerks the needle out, grins.

There. Collapsed.

"One-lung Bethune" they call me in the brasseries of the Old Town!

He puts the machine away, dresses again.

Afraid of death? *Me?* Barney, I intend to die of an overdose of sex at the age of ninety. *Laughs, coughs.* Of course, I'm serious! When I joke – I'm serious! All right, maybe I'm a bit – lost. I thought I was onto something when I went to

Montreal! Surgery for surgery's sake. Cut and be damned. But Christ, Barney – the odds! We need more effective ways of fighting TB. Now – the *cause* of disease – if we could just eliminate that, eh?

You know, there are two kinds of TB. The rich man's TB – and the poor man's. The rich man recovers. The poor man dies. Takes a Depression before that becomes obvious. So why are we scrambling for a cure in the medical lab? Now we have social tools – and we've got to cut out the cause. There *has* to be a way – right? And I have this sense – just an intuition – ever since I left the San – that Bethune is part of it. Oh, I dunno – maybe there's some sort of "cosmic adventure" directing my life. It's really hard on my friends, I know. "Look out for Bethune. A bomb – looking for a place to explode." No, don't deny it! It's true! I know things about myself that people should never know.

He pours another drink, hesitating.

Remember the time I disappeared from the Sanitorium for two days? After the operation – Frances was back then. I got a letter from her in New York – she'd met up with some queer playboy. He was treating her badly. I dunno, looking back – maybe she made all that up. But I went nuts. I always said I was never jealous, but – there I was on the train, going after this chump – planning how to – kill him. *Laughs.* Twenty bucks in my pocket. Spitting slugs of fuscia-coloured snot all over the aisle. Got to town at seven in the morning, up to Harlem, bought a gun. Registered in some hotel. God, I musta looked like a vampire. I rang him up – gave him a phoney name, some "long lost friend from Princeton." *Insisted* he come down to the hotel for a drink. Sat down to wait.

He sits, draws an imaginary gun.

"Come in! No. No mistake. I'm Norman Bethune. Beth. Une. Thaaaaat's right – Frannie's husband. I'm here exterminating pests. *Stands, advances.* So – anything to say? *Nothing?* You did screw her, didn't you? Yes or no? Well, don't just stand there, trembling. Defend yourself! You deserve it? Well, I'll be damned – if – that isn't – the mingiest limp-wristed excuse –

He suddenly strikes him with the "gun."

"So, does that stiffen the old backbone? No?

He hits him several times, starts coughing violently. He hurls the "gun" away.

"Aaaa! Get out! *He calms down.* Come on—get up on your feet. And quit that awful *bawling*! I *hate* cry-babies! Here – sit down. Ah, that's a nasty cut. There.

He extends his scarf.

"God, what a mess."

Well, I couldn't send him down to the lobby looking like that –

He turns back to Barnwell, lights a cigarette.

Anyway, we drank a bottle of Jack Daniels, got into dirty limericks – sent him home in a taxi. Came back on the train that night. So – you see what I mean. Crazy, eh? And I cannot inflict this sort of thing on my friends. My few friends.

Oh, but I thought Montreal was the answer! The gay bachelor's life. Beautiful women – dozens of them. Plenty of hard work. I paint, I teach – even started writing poetry! A good life but – not enough. Still *not enough.*

I think sometimes I'm really an *artist*, trapped in a doctor's body. There I am standing in front of this canvas of living flesh, scalpel and palette in hand. Now you see why my colleagues think I'm dangerous. I am, too. An artist has to *let go* – abandon himself to action. He comes up into the light like some "creature of the monstrous deep" – all jagged and destructive – breaking the smooth surface of mediocrity. And in the banal blare of day, he *enjoys* the purification of violence.

Of course, it's disturbing! The artist's *function* is to disturb! His duty is to rouse the sleeping. To shake the pillars of the world! He must remind humans of their dark ancestry, and still direct them toward a new birth.

I'm no reformer, Barney. I'm a revolutionary! In a world already terrified of change, I preach *revolution*! The principle of life! I am an agitator – a disturber of the excrement – impatient – frightening! I am the creative spirit, liberating the soul of men!

He collapses on the table, drunk.

Barney, where can a guy take a leak?

Scene Five

Bethune is straightening his tie and jacket before a large audience.

Bethune: Ladies and gentlemen, fellow doctors. I speak to you this evening not as a physician, but as a traveller from an antique land. Last August, I went to the forbidden land of Russia – to attend the Physiological Congress, to hear the great Pavlov speak. And I admit, I went to Russia to look at the Russians. I swam in the Neva River, wandered through the streets like any tourist, window-shopping. A combination of Walter Winchell, Peeping Tom and an Innocent Abroad. They told me they'd eliminated prostitution in the workers' paradise, but I was able to prove differently. Propaganda is – after all – propaganda.

But I saw extraordinary things. Impossible things, and while I did not believe all of them, I came away with one unshakable conviction: Socialized Medicine is the only answer to the greatest disease of all – the disease that caused this Depression – the cancer of greed. Greed for wealth. The greed for profit that has entire communities coughing their lungs apart in poisoned air. Monopoly capitalism which promotes the *worst* in human behavior!

Oh yes! Sneer if you like, chum, but the Soviets have found a cure for that cancer! *Extreme*? You bet it is! So is life. So is the creation of new life.

What would a Martian think, watching for the first time a woman in labour? Would he not be appalled at the blood, the agony, the apparent cruelty of the midwife, the whole revolting process of childbirth? He would cry, "Stop this, do something, help, police, murder!" But we'd have to tell him he was seeing magic, that the pain would pass, that the agony and the ugliness were only unrecognized joy and beauty. And what could we say about this woman as she lies there? Is she not ridiculous? – yes: but is she not beautiful? Is she not pitiful, grotesque and absurd? Yes: but is she not magnificent and sublime?

Now Russia is going through such a rebirth, and the doctors have been so busy keeping the precious baby alive that they haven't found time to clean up the mess. And it is this mess, the awkward and sometimes stupid mess, which offends the nostrils of those timid virgins . . . who lack the imagination to see through the blood the significance of birth. Creation never was a genteel sight. It is crude, violent and revolutionary. But to those courageous hearts who believe in the future of man, who divine the power in their own hands, Russia today is the most exciting spectacle since the Renaissance. Deny that and you deny your faith in man!

Scene Six

He is tidying up his apartment.

Bethune: Frances! Hello – oh, I knew you'd come – if I were patient – and asked nicely. How's Coleman? I'm sure you make him very happy. Me? Oh, the usual – a rather interesting affair with the wife of a colleague. She loves to dominate. It's only the danger of it all that keeps the affair going, I'm bound to say. No, beautiful enough, in an aggressive sort of way. None of your charm at all. *Laughs.* Wears a leather nightie to bed.

I asked you to come because – I wanted to tell you – I'm leaving. For Spain. Oh. Nothing. A war. Yes, me! I intend – to fight – these bloody Fascists – however I can. I'm sick of this war – the economic war. In Spain the *real* issues are being fought. There, democracy will live or die.

No – I resigned from the hospital. Settled my debts, or tried to. And I had to buy one huge god-awful case of medical supplies. Took nearly all I had. The bar bill at the press club is just beyond my means. You couldn't stake me to a couple hundred bucks, could you? No, I assure you it was to say farewell. Look, for you.

He presents a red rose.

Day after tomorrow. Empress of Britain. No, I don't suppose we ever can be separated. Our lives are chained together – "for better or for worse." If you could only believe how happy I've been, the last few months, with you living just a few streets away. You still enchant me. I know you think you're immune to all that – even though your eyes – your touch – *Touches her* – your lips – would give you the lie.

You've got to put Bethune and the past behind you, before your memory turns it into something romantic, and threatens to seduce you again. You know as well as I do there's something – self-destructive in me. This fascination with death. I've learned to tolerate that but – not the effect it has on you.

I try to deck you with flowers, and I burden you with my chains! Okay, okay, I know – enough of this. We must have a *merry* leave-taking, smiling our stiff upper lips, but – Frances, don't change! Stay yourself! I'm – always rambling on – like this. Morbid. Should be making you smile. Your rose! Frances . . . ?

He offers the flower, too late. She is gone.

Musician plays and sings: "You Leave, My Love."

You leave my love,
But I must stay behind alone.
Fragments of our dream lie
Shattered round our restless feet.

Did we ask
From heaven more
Than heaven cares
to send down to man?

Now your journey takes us far apart
Does your troubled heart
Beat now for you and me
Or is it beating for a world
I cannot see?

Intermission.

Scene Seven

Bethune is dressed in a Red Cross jacket.

Bethune: *Salud*, Canada! This is Radio Station EAQ, Voice of Spanish Democracy. Norman Bethune reporting from Madrid. Thanks – Canadian *cameradas y companeros* – for the shipment of medicine and bandages. Your medical unit, *Instituto Hispano-Canadiense de Transfusion de Sangre*, has become famous in this bitter war. The first mobile blood transfusions in military history! A thousand transfusions a day, along ahundred-kilometer front.

The carnage here is incredible. Last week, the Fascists started bombing Malaga. The entire population forced to flee two hundred kilometers to Almeria. Hazen Cize and I drove south to help them.

Thousands and thousands – so dense the van can't push through. They flash past our windshields like millions of snowflakes in a blizzard. The old ones give up, lie down in the ditch to wait for death. Children as old as ten slung over their mother's shoulder. Clinging to her hands. Barefoot. A man staggers along with two children on his back, nearly hidden among the pots and pans. Suddenly our van beseiged by a mob of frantic parents. "*Receibeme este*!" "Take the children to Almeria!" Holding out their lifeless arms. Eyes swollen from the dust and sun. "*Este esta herido*!" Blood-stained rags around their limbs. Crying from pain and hunger.

Planes machine-gun the road by day. They tramp all night in a stream of men, goats and children. Crying the names of the lost. "Gustavo! Gustavo!" For three days and nights, we ferry the multitudes, more precious than our bottles of blood, down to Almeria.

But the final barbarism waits. Last night, February 12th, 1937, forty thousand refugees have finally reached sanctuary in the little seaport. Huddled in the main square of Almeria. Sirens begin to wail in the darkness. Mussolini's planes fill the sky. They drop ten huge bombs in the very center of town, which they call a strategic military target. Bodies and limbs fall through the air in a torrent of bloody rain. Three children dead on the pavement in front of the relief office. Killed waiting for a cup of milk. The street a shambles of the dead and dying, lit by the bright orange glare of burning buildings. In the darkness, the screams of children. The curses of men rise in a massive cry, higher and higher. They cry for pity. They cry for revenge. My body heavier than all the dead. Hollow, empty. But in my brain there burns a bright flame of hate.

He sings.

Spanish heavens spread their brilliant starlight
High above our trenches in the plain.
From the distance morning comes to greet us
Calling us to battle once again.
Far off is our land,
Yet ready we stand.
We're fighting and winning for you –
FREEDOM.

This is Norman Bethune signing off in Madrid.

A knock at the door.

Pase adelante! Ah – Mr. McCullum! *Buenos dias* to the Toronto party secretary. *He salutes. No pasaran*! Madrid is truly honoured by your visit. . . .

Pause, then sharply. Oh? What? You must be joking! No! I won't go back to Canada! *Voice rising.* I don't give a damn what the Comintern ordered! Bethune *created* this unit – and he's going to stay until this war is won! How could a Toronto committee understand? *Miracles,* Comrade. We've humanized the face of war! Do you understand, Comrade?

Never mind your dogma-ridden *committee* room? Do I get a say in this "decision?" Our unit was ignored by the "Toronto committee" – never heard from you until the press took notice. Oh – *then* funds rolled in! Well, on this front they value my work – and I'm staying! Of course I understand discipline! *Sharply.* I've read Lenin, thanks! And Trotsky as well! Dammit all, if you want discipline, you start at the top! Each authority issues a hundred and one contradictory orders – and takes no action! It's chaos! They're all trying to seize control of our blood unit – the anarchists, the unions, the communists! God I'd love to put the commissars against the wall and have the bastards shot! I'd do it myself if I wasn't committed to *saving* lives.

I despair of victory in this quicksand of political feuding. You want a new slogan, comrade? "Power is the opiate of the revolutionary class!" I learned one thing here. I'm no general. I'm a guerrilla! I belong at the front, among the bullets and blood. The only part of this war that's *real.* Only in the face of death does life have any meaning!

Look – Mr. McCullum, why don't you go and – tell the committee – Bethune's just too pig-headed to deal with? He refuses to give up his outfit – *Pause.* Well, what the hell am I supposed to do back there? *With great contempt.* Public speaking tour? I know we need funds but there's a Fascist offensive – ! A *direct* order! Well then – I refuse it. Call it what you want! I will not betray the Spanish people.

He throw his fist up in a salute.

No pasarannn!

Scene Eight

Bethune is preparing to address a huge audience. He wears a red tie. He reads from index cards.

Bethune: Ladies and gentlemen, comrades. I am speaking in Saskatoon tonight on behalf of the Committee to Aid Spanish Democracy.

Our purpose is to raise funds for the international struggle against fascism. We hope you will contribute whatever you can afford. Your money will ease the burden of those who are now sacrificing their lives and their limbs, in the struggle for democracy and freedom. The freedom. Of democracy.

My thirty-fourth speech this month. The words are starting to run together. Doesn't make –

Anyway, it's not the money we need, it's to get the truth out – beyond the press. I know one thing from my travelling across this continent. We're all being lied to by the politicians and the newspapers. They're blinding people to the real danger – and all I'm doing is trying to open their eyes.

The papers say Bethune's a communist. Well, who knows? I do believe in the force of history. I try to fight oppression. To see justice served. If that's communism – this country is full of communists. Millions of them. If it's red to be Christian – I am proud to be a red. You see, you can't talk about salvation, without talking revolution. The *idea* of salvation is revolutionary. And I preach for social justice because it's the *poor* who need salvation. I don't just mean the dust-bowl farmers and a generation of young Canadians who have lost hope. I mean, the *world's* poor. The starving billions of Africa and Asia. *Why* do they starve? Not natural disasters. Not "acts of God!" But the greed of rulers – the wealthy few who buy off the middle class and screw the poor. Well, that's all ending. The old Renaissance ideals are gone – individualism – the Great Chain of Being – the supremacy of the white race. To survive on this crowded planet, people have to learn to act together. Co-operatively. United – and not divided.

Right now, we're marching toward another world war. You can see it coming. Inevitable. A death struggle to the finish. Fascism, and the worship of the Individual. Socialism – and the power of the multitudes. You don't have to be red to understand that, friends. It might help to be a doctor, though – because that's all fascism is. A bloody pestilence. And like the dreaded TB, its spread will prove fatal to us all.

We've seen it invade – *points to his chest* – the left lung of Europe. Spain. Where Franco and his German thugs are on the attack. If we don't halt this demonic plague – you and I – the whole free world – then that lung will shrivel and die. Now in the right lung, we are seeing the invasion of China by the Japanese bacillus.

You didn't know about that? No – Asia is ignored by our

blockheaded politicians and their simpering sycophants of the press. Doesn't exist – too poor. One week ago, Japanese soldiers blasted the ancient capital of the world's largest nation – and there wasn't a *peep* out of those freedom-loving, self-appointed saviours of "the free world." Why? Why do they only feel threatened by the Soviet Union? Who is trying to pull the wool over our eyes? Could it be the toadies of the Liberal oligarchy, led by Mackenzie the King? Who's proud to be photographed shaking Adolf's hand?

Well, I'll tell you, friends. Some of you may go to Spain. And the more who go now – to halt these gangsters – the fewer will have to go in the years to come. But I – I am going to China. To the unknown continent, where over half the world lives. There a band of men has organized that is going to beat the Emperor Hirohito back into the sea. One day the world will celebrate this struggle. And Bethune is going to be part of it!

Scene Nine

Bethune is laughing, reading a book.

Bethune: Ever read any Leacock, Jean? Jeannie – you awake?

He holds up book.

Leacock. He wrote about my part of the world. Gravenhurst – Mariposa. Good old Canada! Our country's never had a revolution, you know. Not like here. Or France. The States. Even England had Cromwell. And it's so –

amazing! To be passing through a civilization at its point of ultimate leverage. Even if it is on the slowest goddamn train since the Newfie Bullet! Yeah – laughter. That's what we need in times like these. Hang out for a couple of hours in Smith's Hotel in Mariposa.

He chuckles.

Made me think of Parsons. Our former colleague. I might've gotten to like the old soak if he hadn't run off with our cash when he took one look at Hong Kong! What would Parsons think of Shansi – with his whiskey shakes – his terror of lice? A man with a terminal hangover. We could've taken blood transfusions from his eyeballs!

He laughs.

No, it's not very "amusing," I suppose. Well, if you want amusement, aren't you amused that we've travelled this far – ten thousand miles – and I haven't made one pass at you? My pals would be amused, I can tell you! Well, I did consider it briefly. You're a pretty woman – for a nurse. But – truth is – I've never had an affair with a colleague.

Colleagues' wives – that's different. There was a brain surgeon's wife – a redhead. I have a fatal attraction to you redheads. A different – scent, you know. Anyway, she arranged a rendez-vous on – get this – his operating table. Well, a bit *bizarre* I thought – but safe enough. What I didn't know was that he had a special op scheduled for that night. There we were – full throes of passion – when all the lights came on! I had one hell of a time keeping that one quiet. No. Sex and work should be separate – like church and state. Render unto Venus that which is venereal. . .

He looks at his watch.

Five a.m. Or do they have an a.m. in China?

He leans forward.

What's going to happen when we meet these guys in Yan-an, Jean? I mean, what're they going to say? I'm as nervous as a kid! Talking to the men who made the Long March! No matter what I say, I'll sound like a political innocent! How could *we* understand the politics of a place like this? Or the culture?

Yet . . . I don't know, I seem to remember it from somewhere . . . The people. Temples. Even the famine and disease. Like at Lin Fen, when the Jap planes bombed our mule train? I helped the carters shift a dead mule out of its harness. And I – remembered that. Maybe it was some dead animal I'd strained to lift at Bannock Burn six hundred years ago. You didn't know I was a Scot? Oh yes – the whole black incubus. The doomed Beatons of Scotland. They first showed up on the sacred Isle of Iona, off the Ross of Mull. During the Dark Ages – from Bethune in Normandy. Monks. Herbalists. Magicians of Christianity that St. Columba recruited from France. Physicians in God's service for generations. Then the Vikings in a terrible wave of blood across the Hebrides, slaughtering and looting – and Columba's flame was snuffed. The Beatons survived, a few of them, as fishermen, crofters. And one of them, old John Beaton was brought to the court of James the Sixth and made the royal physician – till he was poisoned by the Scottish lairds. That was the last Beaton doctor, my dear – until me.

But – ah, China is different, isn't it? Different life. Different universe! We arrive with nothing – all our supplies locked up in Hong Kong. Parsons buggering off with the remains of our pitiful sum of money. Nothing but our hands and our minds. And the Chinese welcomed us like the Second Coming. Don't give a damn about our politics. It's our *skills* they respect. It's like they – love us. *He laughs.* And I've rebelled against love all my life! Laughed at it. Cast it off like a bad germ. Now – to come this far – and find myself floating in it, like the sea. . . . It's absurd, isn't it Frances? Hmm? Sorry – *Jean*! Sorry. *Sorry*. Sorry.

Scene Ten

Bethune lights a candle in the darkness.

Bethune: Yes? Who's there? Ah, Tong – what is it? Chairman Mao wants to see *me*? But it's after midnight! No, no – wait. Can we take Jean along too? She's dying to meet him and – it would be a great honour.

Jean! Come on, wake up and grab your boots! We're meeting the great man himself! Tong is here to take us to headquarters. Come on! Forget about a skirt – those pants look fine. This isn't a king you're meeting, it's a guerrilla leader. The man who led the Red Army through the Long March – fighting Nationalist soldiers all the way. Through swamps, over mountains, across every river in the country! They lost over a hundred thousand men! And you know how many made it here to Yan-an? Just ten thousand! But oh God, what men! And women! Now, in these hill-caves in the desert, they've built a revolutionary capital. In just two years! A university, factories, a hospital. I tell you – he's incredible – a genius – a *leader* –

He halts, surprised.

In here? A cave?

Lights change. He enters Mao's presence.

Ni hao, ni hao. We're very well, thank you.

He turns to Tong.

Please tell Chairman Mao that we – Comrade Ewen and I – are very impressed by everything we've seen. We're eager to begin work. I've made a tour of the hospital and I'm afraid I must report that it's badly in need of – yes of course – please translate. Spain? Well, I'm sorry to say there are many problems. Disorganization. Factionalism. The superior weapons of the Fascists. Who? Lorca? No, I never met him. They'd killed him before I got there.

Mr. Chairman, I was at the front. I am a soldier, my job was to save soldiers' lives. That's why I request that you order your generals to assign me to the battle front. To set up mobile blood units, as I did in Spain. If you are not mobilizing medicine, you have troops dying needlessly. In Spain, we operated at the front. Seventy-five percent recovery. Seventy five percent! So if I could just get permission to go to the front –

I see. Yes, the base hospital needs attention. Frankly, if your medical officers took my advice, they'd blow the place up and start all over! Oh yes – the caves are a good defence against aerial bombing but – the dirt! Everywhere. I haven't seen a patient covered with a warm blanket, never mind clean sheets. They sleep on mud *kongs* in their dirty uniforms! You might as well put bullets through their – ! Never mind, don't translate.

Tell Chairman Mao *we* – will start work in the morning. Of course, we'll need a few basics. Pardon? Then who *should* I speak to? The hospital bureaucrats say everything must be approved by "higher authority." And I believe we're speaking to the highest authority in the Eighth Route Army. Right? *Smiles.* Good, that's settled. We're making progress. First, elementary classes in hygiene for all personnel – nurses, doctors, even the cleaners. Second – a power generator for the hospital – for lighting and blood refrigeration. Third! My doctors will need at least two heavy trucks to carry the medical units to the front. In Spain, I had –

What? No doctors? *Pause.* No trucks! *No roads?* Impossible! I'm not a miracle worker! I refuse the assignment! What the hell does this man expect – *everything? Pause.* He does? *Everything?*

He stares at Mao, astonished. He sags for a moment, overwhelmed, then blows the candle out.

Scene Eleven

Bethune writes at a table, wearing glasses.

Bethune: Soong Yen Kou. August, 1938. Hi there Barney, you old sawbones! Well, you should see me now. Nearly fifty, and a soldier once again. Alive and fighting. In fact, I'm embarrassed by longevity! Is it possible that old age will claim Bethune? And wait till you hear about my creature comforts. A typical village in the Wutai Mountains – tiny mud houses, three or four to a family compound. I have a house to myself. One room. A long brick oven called a *kong* runs along one side. It serves as my stove, my bed – and my table. A paper window admits the evening light.

All right, it's a bit rough. But no more than my days in the Ontario bush. Except here we are surrounded by Japanese soldiers. At least they occupy the cities and the railway lines. But we inhabit the enclosing countryside – like sharks in the sea below their little tin boats.

Today, I've been operating since early morning. Exhausted but happy. Who wouldn't be? Doing what I love most cutting and mending.

My doctors are anywhere from nineteen to twenty-two. Peasant boys that I've trained. The nurses are all teen-aged girls. But these people are my greatest resource. They study like crazy, work harder than I do. They listen when I criticize – even put up with my stupid temper.

I've persuaded our commander, General Nieh, to let me build a model hospital here. Better training for my makeshift doctors – close to the fighting. The General is opposed, says a hospital will provoke Japanese attacks. Even so we are rebuilding an old Buddhist temple in a grove of pine and willow trees. Thirty-six beds. When I'm not operating, or teaching, I help the peasants carry stone and timbers. I am awaiting the publication of my new pamphlet, "Hospital Systems in Guerrilla War." Any day now, it'll be out – printed on the backside of Jap propaganda leaflets! Oh, we learn to use everything! It's like the guerrillas' marching song:

Sings.

Mei yo chi, mei yo chuan,
Zi you na diren, song xiang zian
Mei yo qiang, mei yo pao,
Diren gei women zao.

We have no food, we have no clothes,
Ah, but the enemy brings them now.
We have no rifles, we have no guns,
We get them from our foe.

But I do have my bourgeois perks. A cook, my own house, a fine Japanese horse and saddle – a gift from General Nieh. Everything is given that I ask for – except medical supplies.

You must help! Write to the committee in New York. Only seven pounds of catgut left, eight of carbolic acid. I've got two scalpels, a bone chisel and six artery forceps. Distributed the rest. Ten ampoules of morphine. Two kilos of chloroform. When that's gone we cut without anesthetics. Conditions are pitiful: bloody dressings left unburned, food covered with flies. Wounds turn septic in two days. But in the pursuit of victory, we are unstoppable. That's Mao's legacy. These guerrillas know how to unify, how to win people's hearts. The leaders own no possessions, wear the same cotton tunics as my little Red Devil, Tong. The truth is not theoretical, the truth is what *works*. You can't fill a belly or set a broken leg with dogma, Barney. Socialism here is more simple and more complex – it's a way of life! Unconscious as the movement of lungs, relentless as the beating of hearts.

I dream of course. Memories of Montreal, New York, Paris. I dream of coffee, of rare beef, of apple pie and cheddar cheese. Mirages of ordinary food. Books – are books still written? Is music still played? Do you people still dance, drink dark red wine, go to the movies? Do women still love to be loved?

What do you hear from Frances – anything? I've temporarily – lost contact. *Hule la chee snach aichk*. Gaelic – "You see and you don't see." Your old partner. In life and in –

He crosses this word out.

Your old partner – Beth.

Scene Twelve

Bethune is putting on surgical apron. Sound of battle intensifies through scene.

Bethune: All right – what've we got here, Tong? Take the splints off that leg. Phew! Okay – gangrene. Get the chloroform ready, Xiao-hua. We'll have to take it off. You can start washing the leg. Bring two buckets of boiling water!

He lays the instruments out on the table.

Good God! Where has this man been kept? Why do the officers let the wounded lie around *rotting* for three days? What the hell are we *doing* at the front, if we can't get them in here? Hurry up!

To the patient. Tong-jer – ni hao? Laughs. Good. *Hao, hao.* But – lost too much blood. Have to fix it, right now. Tell him we're short of anaesthetic. *Kuai-kuai – dong bu dong?* Okay? Give him a slug of *mao-tai*. It'll hold him for a while. Wait! I'll have one, too. Right. *Gambei.*

He drinks, seizes a saw.

Let's go. Hold him down. Streeeetch it – nice and easy. That's it. See the angle? Now remember – keep these blades sharp. You want to be doctors, you've got to learn the skills of four workers: blacksmith, tailor, carpenter, and butcher. *Starts cutting.* Dammit, hold him down! Tight! Give him the chloroform! Now – cut you bastard – *cut*! Knife! Gimme a knife! Pay attention or I'll have your guts for garters, young lady! *Working.* All right. Fine. Forceps. Good. Another clamp! Right, that's it. Okay, Xiao-hua, finish up the stitching, will you? I need a smoke.

He pulls a battered cigarette from his pocket, steps outside to light it.

Good morning, General. Morning, evening – what's the difference? The guns. Destroy all sense of time. Rest? I can't rest when I'm needed every second. No, I *don't* have to sleep! We operated for sixty-eight straight hours last week at the battle of Chi Hui. A hundred-and-fifteen cases. So I don't think I'm ready for bed yet, General. Oh? Why? Any complaints of negligence? Well, you were right about the hospital. I was wrong – and it broke my heart to see all our work blown to pieces in ten minutes. But that doesn't mean you're right now! I do *not* need to be relieved! My medics are already working twice as hard as I am. What kind of teacher would I be, if I didn't set an example for them?

An *order*? *He laughs shortly.* Well, I can't disobey an order, can I, General?

He flops down on the ground.

All right, here I am. Lying down. Resting. You don't mind if I smoke?

He smokes furiously until even he feels ridiculous. He flings the cigarette and leaps to his feet.

Dammit, this is ridiculous! How can a guy sleep with a battle going on a mile away? General, I came here to serve the people. That's what Chairman Mao wanted. Now, are you gonna let me serve the people or not? Never mind "orders!" Exhaustion is a medical question, right? Not a military question. And in the medical command, I issue the orders, not you. So I'm giving an order. Bethune – get back to the operating table!

Look – another soldier going in. See that arm? My men can cut that off. But they can't set it. Do you want that man to carry a rifle again, General? Tong – I'll take that patient!

Scene Thirteen

Bethune is exhausted, in a trance.

Bethune: The kerosene lamp overhead makes a steady buzzing sound like an incandescent hive of bees. Mud walls. Mud floor. Mud bed. Smell of blood and chloroform. Cold. Three o'clock in the morning. Men with wounds. Wounds like dried pools, caked with earth; wounds with torn edges filled with black gangrene; wounds, expanding outward, decaying orchids or crushed carnations, terrible flowers of flesh.

Old filthy bandages stuck to the skin with blood-glue. Careful. Gangrene's such a cunning, creeping fellow. Better moisten first. Through the thigh. Pick the leg up. Like a big, loose, red stocking. A Christmas stocking. Where's that fine, strong rod of bone now? In a dozen pieces. Pick them out with your fingers: white as dog's teeth, sharp and jagged.

Is this one alive? Give him saline intravenously. Perhaps the tiny cells of his body will remember the hot, salty sea, their ancestral home, the first flood. With the memory of a million years, they may recall other tides, other oceans, life born of the sea and sun.

And this one. Will he run along the road beside his mule at another harvest? No, never again. How can he run with one leg?

How beautiful the body is; how perfect its parts; with what precision it moves; how obedient, proud and strong. How terrible when smashed. The little flame of life sinks lower and lower, and goes out like a flickering candle. Quietly. Silent.

More men with wounds? Four Japanese prisoners. Bring them in. No enemies in this community of pain, no strangers among these torn bodies. Cut away that blood-stained uniform. Stop that haemorrhage. Lay them beside the others. Why, they're alike as brothers! Are these professional man-killers? No, they are amateurs-in-arms. Workman's hands. Careful. Come round now! The other side! Chisel! *Takes a bone chisel.* Now. One sharp break – here! *Ahhhh*!

He seizes his left hand, covered with blood, gazing at it in wonder.

Musician plays and sings "Beyond the Yellow River."

Red sun burning in the east
Beyond the Yellow River Plain.
People's dreams of ever-lasting peace
Caress this ancient land like mist
Softly falling rain
Does red blood glisten in sun?
Does peace demand
The price of so much pain?

Scene Fourteen

Bethune is lying on the floor, shivering from the cold. He holds his left arm as though in a sling, trying to undress.

Bethune: Frances? Is that you, Frances? Ah, Tong. Did you mail the letters? Where's my bag?

Never treated it. *Stupid.* After all my shouting at the others. Look at my armpit. Abscess big as an egg. Chills. Fever. Temperature's forty degrees. Christ – that's it. Septicemia. Frances! Is that you?

Looks around. Who are all these people, Tong? Ask them to go away. Well, don't they know it's rude to stare? A man needs privacy on certain occasions – shitting – dying. Anyway, Frances may come. Okay, okay – let them stay. Can't make much difference now. Maybe I'll do better with an audience.

Need more time to – mobilize the blood unit – few more men – *companeros* – no, can't go back – all politics! Ah, there you are, darling, my angel –

He stares in horror.

Not you, you black bitch! Get away! Not yet! Go on!

Ah, *ma cherie*, I knew you'd come. What do you think, darling, shall we march to the altar one more time? Third time lucky, they say. *Chuckles.* Say, you couldn't spot me a few bucks – just till payday? Oh yes, I'll admit you're a prophet. "Beth – you'll never be happy until you die the death of an obscure martyr!" It was only that *obscure* bit I really objected to.

But that is my fate, isn't it? I am a Beaton, after all – full of violence and stubbornness. Intolerant. But with it all, a vision of some truth – even when it leads, as it did for my ancestors, to an early grave. I have known it since that spring of our romantic folly in Edinburgh. I travelled out to the Hebrides, to the Ross of Mull – I wanted to unlock – the mystery of my beginnings. Very little there – a few derelict stone huts, the name Beaton carved above the door. All of them evicted decades ago. Except for one blind old woman – the last of the Beatons. We sat in silence while the clock ticked in her kitchen. Finally she spoke – asked if I were a doctor. I could – see myself – reflected in her blank eyes. I said I was a – poet. But her stream of tears made me a liar. She gave me her cross – the cross of St. Columba.

He pulls it from his shirt.

My comrades here believe it's a magic amulet – to keep demons away. And after all those years of – acquisition, it's the only thing I have. All my paintings. Books. Books. My fine clothes. Naked as Lazarus.

He shivers violently, lies down on table.

Tong. *Tong*. Put coal on the fire. Tong – Listen. Instructions . . . We need – 250 pounds of quinine, 300 of iron compounds. The manual. Printing. Next week. By the typewriter. Mobile units – operating.

Barney! Tell them – I have been happy. These two years – the greatest of – my life. Now – Chairman Mao needs – me –

Pause.

Frances? Frannie! Ah – you – darling. In thy – soft – arms at – last –

Bethune dies on the table, lying as he was at the beginning. Lights fade to black.

The End

The Great Cultural Revolution

Playwright's Introduction: Wu Han

Wu Han, the hero of *The Great Cultural Revolution*, was a very different kind of rebel than Davin and Bethune. And to understand his relationship to history, a brief account of modern Chinese politics will be useful.

Forty years before the recent tragedy in Tiananmen Square, the People's Liberation Army marched into Beijing to the adulation of the entire Chinese nation. There was no mistaking their loyalty. Under Mao Zedong, they put the final stamp on the Chinese Revolution after twenty years of bloody civil war. The largest - and oldest - country in the world suddenly "turned" Communist under the nervous eyes of the newly formed United Nations of the world.

Mao and his officials, notably Premier Zhou Enlai and Army Chief Peng Dehuai, wasted no time in deconstructing the old landlord system, redistributing farm land to the peasants who had been the backbone of his revolution. New standards were set in health, education, and industrial production. For the first time in history, 400,000,000 Chinese women ceased to be chattels. Almost immediately the Chinese army was drawn into the Korean War, provoked by General Douglas MacArthur's invasion.

General Peng become a military hero in Korea by fighting the U.N. armies to a standstill, while waves of fear swept the globe about the yellow hordes of "Red China."

Chairman Mao Zedong's first Five-Year Economic Plan was a resounding success, so impressive that he immediately proclaimed the "Great Leap Forward" campaign in 1958. The emphasis turned to massive agricultural communes and radical decentralization ("peasantizing") of industrial production. The peasants began constructing a vast array of primitive backyard iron foundries, and surrendering their recently secured land into the commune system.

Mao's enormous popularity carried the plans forward, with ever-increasing exhortations from the cadres for "more effort, more sacrifice." The peasants had been liberated by his revolution, and they kept responding to the calls.

Unfortunately, bad weather and a number of flaws in Mao's plan opened a crack in the dream. Hundreds of thousands of people starved to death when the crops failed. The backyard smelters became a cruel joke, producing useless heaps of melted iron. At the Lushan conference in 1959, Marshall Peng dared to criticize the Great Leap Forward. He was immediately fired, and a serious split opened in the Chinese Communist Party. Mao resigned as head of state, but his program went forward under President Liu Shaoqi and party secretary Deng Xiaoping, somewhat more cautiously. The general public still saw Mao as the man in charge. In fact it was during this period that the Thoughts and Badges of Mao became all-pervasive. Dissent went underground.

Wu Han was a highly regarded bureaucrat, and uncharacteristically for a vice-mayor of Beijing, not a Communist Party member. He was also a widely-published Professor of History at Beijing University. Within a few weeks of Marshall Peng's dismissal, he began working on his play (actually a Beijing opera) called *Hai Rui's Dismissal*. It was produced in 1960 and published in January, 1961.[1] The parallels between Peng's fall and this drama about Hai Rui were immediately obvious to Chinese intellectuals. In China, *everything* is political, but in 1960 (after the notorious "Hundred Flowers Campaign" of 1957), language was very carefully used. His play was full of references to land seizure, and criticism of the emperor. The opera became a subject of intense analysis and local gossip – and it wasn't long before an assault began on Wu Han and his collaborators (and defenders, like President Liu and Deng

Xiaoping). This spark ignited the firestorm that became the "Great Proletarian Cultural Revolution" – a civil war that engulfed the entire country.

The first volley was fired by "the Gang of Four" from Shanghai in November, 1965, and the barrage quickly intensified. Within six months the Red Guards were attacking "old culture, old ideas" and promoting Jiang Qing's (Madame Mao's) six revolutionary operas as the only acceptable theatre entertainment. The following ten "years of turmoil" not only masked a struggle for power within the CCP, but unleashed the Red Guard movement, a kind of children's crusade against Communist authority. It was a stunning spectacle, of great fascination to the Western media who had no idea *what* was going on, and it became the symbolic model for the international student uprisings of the 1960s. The Red Guards inspired a legion of imitators from the Bader-Meinhof gang to the Japanese Red Army Faction – and ironically the Democracy movement that nearly torched Beijing twenty-three years later.

Youthful cadres, mainly recruited among the educated élite, attacked the Confucian and "capitalist past" by assaulting their teachers and informing on their parents. The movement villifed the "stinking intellectuals" until the universities finally closed. By 1970, the GPCR had devastated millions of lives. Economically, the country regressed ten years. It is still called the Disastrous Decade in China. And the scars have remained long after.

I was impressed that a mere drama could have such powerful consequence, and determined to learn more about the playwright Wu Han, who died in 1969, apparently driven to suicide.

"The ancients had a proverb," he wrote in the preface to his play, "'Throw a brick to get a gem.' That is to say that this drama should be taken as 'the throwing of a brick' to stimulate interest of my friends in the field of history. Perhaps they will all come forward and write a new historical drama."[2]

And who was Hai Rui, Wu Han's allegorical hero? Hai Rui was a "just official," a historical figure of the Ming period who has appeared in many plays and stories in China. He became known as a righteous public servant who defended the common people and would not be bullied by the Ming emperor, his one-time friend. In literature, he personifies Confucian principles of honour, decency, and justice. A sort of Chinese, well – Norman Bethune.

Hai Rui is an unlikely rebel, but then so was Peng Dehuai – and Wu Han himself. Chinese history and legend is full of unlikely rebels, all the way back to Monkey, the clever trickster-hero of *Journey to the West*, who led the monkeys' rebellion against the Emperor of Heaven. Peasant revolutionaries were renowned long before Mao Zedong's ascent to power. The first Ming Emperor, Zhu Yuanzhang, was a peasant who led a rebellion in 1368 and founded the most civilized of the fabled dynasties of The Middle Kingdom.

Wu Han wrote, "Dare to think, dare to speak, dare to do has been the new style since the Great Leap Forward. I wrote a drama. Thus I belong to the ranks of those who dare. If I did not dare, then I simply could not do anything successfully. . . . As for the magnitude of the achievement, or whether it is a success or failure, that is another thing. The historical development of a human society is also simply the history of people who dare to think, dare to speak, and dare to do."[3]

Wu Han would not have had time in July, 1966, to produce his over-publicized play as a defence against the growing criticism (as *The Great Cultural Revolution* hypothesizes), but the dramatic possibilities of a play-within-a-play outweigh strict historical accountability. *The Great Cultural Revolution* is, after all, about hard political choices, when Wu Han discovers he is in the same boat as his heroes Hai Rui and Peng Dehuai. He must go to the wall.

The playwright as tragic hero – doomed by his own faith in the power of the word – naturally appeals to another playwright. It's certainly not the average entertainment playing in Canadian theatres now. Drama has become politically irrelevant, ideas virtually banned. Too many of our playwrights have become political eunuchs, purveying psychobabble and pandering to sentimentality, trying to get to Broadway. In Czechoslovakia in 1989, Vaclav Havel rode Wu Han's tiger to a happier conclusion, but that is another story, revealing much about the contradictions between West and East.

It was courageous of Vancouver's Arts Club Theatre to première this epic play in 1979, directed by Brian Richmond. David Liang's ***kunchu*** opera music was a success from its opening theme. In retrospect I can't believe that we had a cast of sixteen, including acrobats and musicians – but it happened. In those days we were witnessing the start of a "cultural revolution" in Canadian theatre and big things seemed eminently possible.

As with all revolutions, only history will judge.

---

1. Clive Ansley, *The Heresy of Wu Han*, University of Toronto Press: Toronto, 1971, p. 113.
2. Ibid. p. 9.
3. Ibid. p. 9.

Nicholas Rice as Li Chen, Alec Willows as Yao Hanlin, Arts Club Theatre, Vancouver, 1979.

First Performance

The Great Cultural Revolution was premièred at the Arts Club Theatre, Vancouver, in November 1979, under the direction of Brian Richmond, with music composed by David M.Y. Liang, choreography by Kaz Pieswocki, musical direction by Bruce Kellet, and design by Alison Green. The cast was as follows:

Tang Tianmei – *Christine Anton*
Bi Weimin – *Edward Astley*
Chang Xiao – *Guy Bannerman*
Lin Hulan – *Sherry Bie*
Wu Han – *Michael Fawkes*
Ning Rulan – *Jill Diane Filion*
Zhou Suchen – *Edward Greenhalgh*
Feng Baoda – *Richard Newman*
Li Chen – *Nicholas Rice*
Hu Chungfa – *Colin Thomas*
Yao Hanlin – *Alec Willows*
Musicians – *Graeme Boyle, Norman Stanfield, Ben Neumann*
Acrobats – *Anne Brunner, Alan Limbert*

The author gratefully acknowledges the first translation into English of *Hai Rui's Dismissal* by Clive Ansley of the University of Windsor: *The Heresy of Wu Han*, University of Toronto Press, 1971.

Characters

Wu Han: The author and now the director of *Hai Rui's Dismissal.* He was formerly a deputy mayor of Beijing and a professor of history of Beijing University. About fifty years old. He plays *Hai Rui.*

Zhou Suchen: Caretaker of the theatre, a former peasant and soldier, 70. He plays *Xu Fu.*

Hu Chungfa: A professional actor, 40. He plays *Xu Ying.*

Tang Tianmei: A professional actress and assistant director, 40. She plays *Hong Alan.*

Li Chen: Secretary of the Academy of Drama, 45. Also an actor and dedicated Communist. He plays *Xu Jie.*

Chang Xiao: A reluctant actor. He plays *Zhao Youshen*, *Li Pingdu* and *Dai Fengxiang.*

Ning Rulan: A student actress, 18. She plays *Zhao Xiaolan* and *Wang Shi.*

Bi Weimin: A graduate history student, 20. He plays *Wang Mingyou.*

Yao Hanlin: A stage hand and technician. He plays *Peasants.*

Lin Hulan: Leader of the Red Flag faction of Red Guards at Beijing Teachers' College, 20. She plays *Announcer.*

Feng Baoda: Red Guard from Fu Dan University, Shanghai.

Musicians: In army uniform.

Setting

A small theatre at the Central Academy of Drama in Beijing. August, 1966.

Act One

The lights come up on Zhou Suchen, sweeping on stage with a broom and dustpan. It is quite dirty, littered with scripts, ashtrays, cigarette butts, etc. Overlooking all, on the rear bare wall of the stage, is a huge portrait of Chairman Mao Zedong, like an icon. There are posters stuck up all over, which proclaim in large bold characters: "Long Live Chairman Mao!" "Carry Forward the Proletarian Revolution" "Art Must Serve the People." A couple of cruder, new posters, state: "Bombard the Party Headquarters!" "Attack the Four Olds!" "Let Politics Take Command!"

Zhou is a cheerful, expressive old man, who shows obvious irritation when cleaning up someone's personal mess. He suddenly strikes a pose and sings.

Zhou: When old men are treated like dogs,
Even Heaven must be offended!

He strikes another dramatic pose.

My tortured body shall be avenged,
My kidnapped child defended. . . .

A door slams offstage somewhere, and he hastily begins sweeping again. Tang Tianmei enters with a bicycle briskly.

Tang: Good morning, Comrade Zhou. How are you?

Zhou: The same.

Hands of ice and feet of pain,
but you'll never hear old Zhou complain!

Tang: *Laughs.* Better today, then. Anyone here yet?

Zhou: How would I know? I don't count noses, I only sweep up after the "stars."

Tang: *Looking around.* We told them nine o'clock.

Zhou: And here it is, nine-fifteen. These actors are all the same – sleep till noon if they had the chance.

Tang: *Defensive.* Well – I was delayed by traffic.

Zhou: Lazy as dogs. A few months feeding chickens on a commune would cure that.

Tang: Has Professor Wu arrived?

Zhou: *Gesturing.* In the office. "Meditating."

Tang: Hmm. I don't suppose there's any water for tea?

Zhou: She doesn't suppose there's any water for tea! What am I, a canteen cook, to keep you parasites drowned in tea? Boil your own water! And get your muddy feet off my work area!

Tang laughs and starts backstage. She meets Hu Chungfa, a handsome actor who plays romantic leads. He is out of breath.

Tang: Good morning, Hu.

Hu: Yes, yes, I suppose.

Tang: You can slow down. We're the first ones here.

Hu: We'll be the only ones!

Tang: Oh? Why?

Hu: Well – the streets are crawling with "Red Guards!" Gangs of them! You didn't notice?

Zhou: Those kids need their asses paddled, if you ask me.

Hu: Is the Professor here?

Tang: In the back?

Hu: *Confidentially.* You think the rehearsal will be cancelled?

Tang: Don't be silly. How about getting the water for tea? It looks like we'll be late getting started.

Hu: What a life! Romantic lead to tea-boy in one week! *Exits.*

Zhou: *Calling.* And don't forget to wash the cups! *Mutters.* Aaa – a waste of breath! Just like pigs.

Tang walks back across the stage, looking for someone.

Zhou: Watch where you're walking! Look at that! Ploughing right through the dirt!

Tang: I'm sorry. Where's Yao? *Comrade Yao!*

Yao Hanlin, the theatre technician, pops out of the set somewhere, perhaps down from the light grid. He looks harassed and busy.

Yao: What is it?

Tang: When can we start?

Yao: Ha! You'll be lucky!

Tang: Lucky?

Yao: The bastards are staying away in hordes! Your actors!

Tang: Oh, they'll come. We might have to wait a few minutes – the streets are so chaotic.

Yao: Wait a few minutes! *Mutters.* And what would happen if you had to "Wait a few minutes" for the comrade technician? Ha. The screams I'd hear . . . !

Tang: You have a formal complaint?

Yao: Nothing, Comrade Director! *Smiles.* Not at all. No problems! We have ten people to do a play written for forty characters. No one to fix the lights. And now I have to read lines as well. . . .

He walks off-stage, muttering. Zhou rips down a couple of the crude posters from the walls.

Zhou: Who are these Red Guards, anyway? Sticking these things up all over the place. Why aren't they in classes, studying the Revolution?

Tang: *Patiently.* They're carrying forth Chairman Mao's new revolution, Comrade Zhou.

Zhou: Bah! What do they know about revolution? They were all sucking on their mothers' tits when we drove the fascists out of Beijing! Aaa! I can't follow what's happening any more. The university is *covered* with posters, and none of them make sense! "Rebellion is justified!" "Bombard the Party Headquarters!" "Attack the Four Olds!" What a lot of whining from the babies. In the old days, we'd have shipped them off to Jiangsu to tend pigs.

Bi Weimin and Chang Zongwen enter, arguing.

Chang: And if they find us doing this play, we'll be more than criticized!

Bi: The correct procedure is to discuss it with our fellow workers –

Tang: *Relieved.* Ah, at last.

Chang: Whew! Wait till you hear what happened!

Zhou: If Chang made it, the others *must* be coming!

Chang: We're lucky to be alive! A gang of Red Guards stopped us in West Chang-an Street.

Bi: They were throwing some "reactionaries" out of an apartment block. He was lucky I was with him.

Chang: Like a typhoon! Throwing furniture into the street, burning it. Books – pictures – even bird-cages . . .

Tang: *A bit shocked.* What were they looking for?

Bi: Any remnants of feudal thinking. The Four Olds.

Chang: Old men – dragged down the street with dunce caps on their heads. Placards round their necks.

Bi: Quit worrying. They're only searching out former landlords and capitalists, really. Everyone is turning them in!

Chang: "Revolution forever!" All the antique pottery is being smashed!

Bi: They let us go when I mentioned I was a member of the March

9th Brigade.

Tang: All right – go and get some tea. Don't bother with costumes. We have to start right away.

Chang: *Alarmed.* You're not going ahead, are you? This play would be the end of us! I only came in to –

Bi: Comrade Tang – the situation has changed. This whole project of Professor Wu's needs serious re-examination.

Chang: Who would come, in the midst of this turmoil? Only the radical factions! We're just making trouble for ourselves!

Tang: This issue has been discussed a dozen times. We all agreed. The course is fixed.

Zhou: He's terrified these kids will come and see him in an old-style play!

Chang: Well, what if I am a bit cautious? I'm not the only one. Where's the rest of our brave cast? All dropped out!

Tang: They'll be here. *Patiently.* Now go and get ready.

Chang and Bi go back stage.

Chang: I knew we shouldn't have come! But no, you and your "great debates" . . .

Zhou: *Singing to himself.*

> Rats, rats, are everywhere,
> Running down the ropes,
> Clinging to the rafters,
> Chewing up our hopes. . . .

Tang: Yao – did none of the students come?

Yao: *Popping out again.* Not a one, Director Tang. Fewer of them every day.

Tang: *Exasperated.* They know how important this is!

Zhou: They're all scared of those Red Guards, terrorizing old people. Bullies!

Yao shrugs as Li enters, looking grim and determined.

Zhou: Well, look who's here – the head cadre himself.

Tang: Comrade Li! Thank heavens! Nothing but trouble this morning.

Li: The political situation is turning hot.

Tang: He's preparing changes to the script.

Li: I've just come from a meeting at the City Office! Shanghai's waging an all-out attack on Professor Wu's play! The Guards have found out it's being presented somewhere at the university, and there's wall posters going up all over, denouncing us! They say the play attacks "Certain People!"

Tang: Ridiculous! Professor Wu's revolutionary reputation is unblemished.

Li: I'm reporting what they said. Thousands of Guards are pouring into the city! We have to be ready for anything.

Tang: *Uncertainly.* Well, we could have a discussion before we begin. *Checks her watch.* If it's brief. You know he hates delays –

Li: I'd better go and warn him –

Tang: No!

Li: This is a political matter!

Tang: He can decide when he comes in.

The musicians enter, in army uniform.

Tang: Yao. The musicians are here! Where's the percussionist?

Li goes out. The musicians shrug.

Yao appears.

Yao: What is it, Director Tang?

Tang: We may need you in percussion, too.

Yao: Is that the best the army could do? A chamber trio?

Tang: So it appears. Are the lights fixed?

Yao goes off, grumbling. Zhou comes smartly to attention and salutes with his broom.

Zhou: Stage cleaned and ready for action, Director.

Tang: Good work, comrade. Could you stay around for a while? It seems we may be a bit short-handed.

Zhou: Oh yes? A part? For extra work points, you mean?

Tang: Yes, yes, all right.

Chang, Hu and Bi re-enter, with bits of costume and makeup.

Bi: No, no – the correct procedure is further discussion – revolutionary debate.

Chang: It's trouble, no matter which way we turn.

Bi: The wall-posters claim Chairman Mao supports them!

Hu: I don't want to hear about wall-posters!

Tang: Quiet! Professor Wu will have something important to say. Where is Lin Xia?

Chang: Last night, he said he was feeling very ill, and we might have to go ahead without him.

Zhou: Ha! Quivering like a piece of bean-curd!

Hu: How can we go ahead without the major actor? I say, we chuck it.

Bi: Besides, it's too old-fashioned! People want *revolutionary* operas these days.

Li re-enters.

Li: What's all the noise about? *To Tang.* Can't you maintain discipline?

Tang: You want discipline? Then you take charge – !

Li: *Backing off.* No, no. I'm only here to advise.

Hu: Advise? If the party took my advice, this whole venture would be cancelled. Right now! It's too – political.

Li: Oh? And are you an authority on politics, or are you a rotting piece of dogshit – ?

Tang: *Be quiet!*

The group falls silent.

Tang: You are acting like children. Comrade Zhou, please call the Professor.

Zhou salutes and goes off-stage.

Chang: So. Another vote?

Li: No more votes! This play has been authorized by the Cultural Revolutionary Group of the City Committee.

Bi: The posters call it a "big poisonous weed!"

Chang: It's obviously political!

Hu: Cultural workers have no business in politics!

Li: Idiot! Your work *is* politics!

Wu Han and Zhou enter. Wu Han carries his script and a copy of Mao's Quotations, *a small red book.*

Zhou: "Enter the tiger, the jackals fall silent."

Wu Han: Good morning. I am glad you all came, despite the – difficulties. *Smiles.* It seems I am becoming a famous playwright. Not bad for a history professor's first play.

Bi: It's a good play, Professor. Nobody doubts –

Wu Han: So this criticism shouldn't be a surprise. Yet my critics aren't attacking its dramatic shortcomings, but its politics. It is "historically inaccurate." It "betrays the class struggle."

Chang: *Sotto voce.* He's going ahead!

Wu Han: Well, I may be an amateur in the theatre, but I know something about history. As to politics, well – we will let the audience decide. In my opinion and, *gestures to Li*, others; it is a revolutionary drama, which "serves the people." It has the support of the city committee, and the Central Academy of Drama.

Li: We'll draw the ultra-leftists into the open.

Hu: Will we get heroes' wreaths on our graves?

Bi: The Red Guards say it's an attack on the Revolution!

Li: A few leftist reactionaries have duped the revolutionary youth movement, that's all.

Chang: But there are ***millions*** of them!

Wu Han: No matter. We have the personal approval of Mayor Peng Zhen and even more senior officials.

Hu: Fat lot of good they'll do. They're all being targetted, too!

Li: Professor Wu, I've just come from the City Committee, and they urge us to press ahead. An army platoon has been assigned to our protection.

Tang: *What?*

Wu Han: But we never requested it! Who decided?

Li: Well – the committee. I came straight here. Why, what's wrong?

Chang: What good's a *platoon*? There are *millions* of them.

Wu Han: This changes everything. Our whole point was in waging a cultural struggle! A violent confrontation means *defeat*!

Li: *Carefully.* With all due respect, Professor, we've passed the point of philosophical debate. There's a political showdown in the making. Both the Committee and the higher authorities are determined to stop the excesses of the Red Guards.

Chang: And we're the battlefield?

Li: Everyone is being attacked by these leftists. Last week the President of China! Today, even Zhou Enlai!

Bi: The Guards say they are carrying out the orders of Chairman Mao.

Tang: Who knows? Who *are* these Red Guards, anyway?

Zhou: Kids wrapped in red flags.

Bi: They're the Chairman's personal creation – radical youth to spearhead the Great Proletarian Cultural Revolution. There are brigades springing up all over China.

Li: I tell you, they're being misled by ultra-left reactionaries. *Pointedly.* The Shanghai faction.

Tang: Ah.

Hu: But *why* do they hate the play?

Chang: The posters say it "glorifies ghosts and emperors and monsters from the past," and is therefore anti-proletarian.

Tang: What nonsense!

Bi: There's more. Now they say the play defends the traitor Peng Dehuai!

Chang: Who?

Li: What?

Bi: Peng Dehuai – the traitorous villain Chairman Mao fired in 1959.

Tang: Is there anything in that? Professor Wu?

Li: It's a plot to stir the army up. They're using the Chairman's name falsely!

Hu: Thank you, Professor Wu.

Wu Han: No. Our play is not a defence of Peng Dehuai! It is a defence of criticism. What are these people afraid of? They find conspiracy behind every metaphor! There are a hundred situations which could parallel this story – and all of them, or *none* of them might be true. That is the power of art! And why we must present this play!

If the fanatics crush me and my play, they will go on to bigger and bigger targets. This is our struggle – the struggle of artists! We have the support of our country's responsible leaders, and we must not capitulate to the mob! Our production will be a victory for the Chinese Revolution.

Chang: Nobody said anything about victory when this thing was proposed! We didn't know what we were getting into – !

Li: The same old whine. Come on. We're losing time.

Tang: Some comrades feel there should be further discussion, Professor Wu –

Wu Han: You agree, Tianmei?

Tang: No, I support you fully but – Lin Xia hasn't turned up, either. *Pause.* We could postpone for a few days. Till the furore dies down.

Li: Absolutely not!

Chang: Just till things cool off.

Tang: More than Red Guards object to the play. You must read the newspapers.

Li: They've fallen under the control of Shanghai!

Tang: The newspapers set down the Party line. And this drama does not conform to the line – which is why our actors, and even the students, are afraid to come. It makes me nervous too.

Wu Han: Well, the Party line has been known to change. And perhaps it will change if people actually *see* this play, and explore the issues. It is the only way. People fear a thing only when they do not understand.

Chang: Fine. Well, let's wait till they change the party line, *then* we can do it.

Li: No. At 4 p.m. tomorrow, there will be a staged reading of

HuRui's Dismissal in this lecture theatre – as advertised!

There is a commotion off-stage. A door is slammed. Ning Rulan, an attractive young student, runs in, out of breath.

Zhou: Here's Ning Rulan!

Tang: What's wrong?

Ning: Red Guards! We stopped – at the canteen - for a bean roll. Someone told them - we were students - in the play. One of them knew about it! They chased us!

Hu: Chased you? Here?

Chang: Now we'll all be shot!

Ning: It's all right! They're not from Beijing! Didn't know their way around. Some soldiers stopped them outside the main building.

Li: Good. The army unit is in place.

Tang: Professor Wu, we have a right to know what is going! What's the army doing here?

Chang: Another vote! We should have another vote!

Wu Han: Comrades - in a time of confusion, we fall back on our principles – the discipline of the Revolution, and the discipline of our art. Chairman Mao's directives on the Cultural Revolution have not been very clear. People don't know which action is revolutionary, which is counter-revolutionary. Which is right, which is left.

Hu: That's true!

Chang: My opinion, exactly.

Wu Han: The Red Guards believe they are revolutionary, because they are rebelling against authority. But in the history of the Chinese people, their out-bursts are a few seconds of passing hysteria.

Bi: Contradiction! Chairman Mao calls the Red Guards his disciples, and he is the living symbol of the Revolution.

Wu Han: Perhaps. But the Chairman also said, "Contradiction is the backbone of revolution."

Hu: What's this got to do with the performance?

Wu Han: What we need – in a time of anarchy – is principled action! And my drama is the portrayal of such a man – Hai Rui! People can look to his example.

Hu: I'm only an actor, not a political scientist.

Li: You are a fool!

Wu Han: What was the cry of the Great Leap Forward?

Zhou: "*Dare*!"

Wu Han: "Dare to think, dare to speak, dare to do!" Could we have stronger direction than that from Chairman Mao? We are presenting a hero who *dared*! We too must dare. There is no distinction between politics and art. In our art, we make our stand. *Points to poster.* Remember – "Art must serve the people!"

Yao: It's ten o'clock, Director Tang.

Tang: Is the discussion over? *Pause.* Once again, the vote. For proceeding?

Li, Yao, Tang, Ning, and Musicians immediately raise their arms. Bi, Hu and Chang then follow. Zhou and Wu Han observe.

Hu: Well, we still don't have enough.

Tang: I also asked Comrade Zhou to help, Professor. Just in case.

Wu Han: Lin Xia is not here?

Tang: "Sick."

Wu Han: Then we'll follow our contingency plan. The students can read the peasants – and I will perform the role of Hai Rui. All right?

Zhou: Not enough to be the author – now he has to play the lead!

Tang: Don't you think it might look rather – strange?

Hu: She means, unprofessional.

Wu Han: It is the story that's important, not the spectacle of the acting. Now – *pause* – Chang Zongwen.

Chang: Yes?

Wu Han: You will read three roles: the grandfather, the prefect and the new governor.

Chang: *Pleased.* Really?

Wu Han: Yes. You can be both victim and villains.

Hu: He can have my part, too, if he wants.

Wu Han: The other students will be here tomorrow, if the army does its job. In the meantime, the part of Xu Fu will be read by Zhou!

Everyone is shocked, turns to stare at Zhou.

Zhou: *Startled.* Eh? *What?*

Bi: The janitor?

Chang: Ridiculous!

Hu: We'll be laughed out of the academy.

Tang: It's not a bad idea. If we all agree.

Wu Han: It's the only solution for today. Will you do it, Zhou?

Zhou: Well, I dunno. Do I get to wear a silk robe?

Wu Han: *Laughs.* If you like.

Tang: *To the others.* He can do it. He's in here clowning every day, anyway. And all he has to do is read the script. You *can* read, can't you?

Zhou: *Proudly.* Two thousand characters!

Li: Well. He couldn't be worse than some.

Ning: What do you say, Comrade Zhou?

Zhou: Sure! I'll do anything for the Revolution. I've been through it all: The Shanghai Massacre, the Long March. I tell you, I was there when we kidnapped Chiang Kai-shek!

And I carried a machine gun the day we liberated Beijing! There is *nothing* I can't do: peasant, soldier, worker – even actor. It's all the same to Zhou Suchen!

Wu Han: We could all learn from Comrade Zhou.

Zhou: Just one question. Who gets to be the sweeper?

Wu Han: I beg your pardon?

Zhou: Well, that's the deal, isn't it? Zhou is promoted to actor – someone else is promoted to floor sweeper. How else would the work get done?

Wu Han: A good point. Volunteers?

He looks around at the actors. They raise their hands, one after another. Yao does not. All the others look at him. Muttering, he raises his arm.

Thank you. *Everyone* is now a janitor. Please don't forget. *To Zhou.* Here – I've marked the script for you. Xu Fu, the bumbling servant.

Zhou: Right, let me see. . . . *Studies the script.*

Tang: All set? Let's go.

Yao: Places everyone.

With remarkable discipline, the actors take their places. Yao puts Zhou in stage position. Lights dim. Music of "the play" begins.

Wu Han: *Hai Rui's Dismissal From Office*, a Kunchu opera!

Yao: Huating County, in the year 1569. The season of the Ching-Ming Festival.

Tang enters as Hong Alan, *and Ning as her daughter,* Zhao Xiaolan – *two peasants. They carry incense and paper money for burning over the graves of their dead.*

Tang: *Sings.*

During the Ching-ming Festival,
We honour the graves of the dead –
Full of grieving and sorrow
Since I lost the husband I wed.

Tang: *Speaks.* Light the incense, Xiaolan. Burn the money over your dear father's grave. If the gods hear our prayers, they might take pity.

Tang and Ning: *Singing.*

Husband (Father), you slaved away for years,
Ploughing fields by night and day,
Paying taxes, finding no rest,
Until the devils took you away!
Landlord Xu seized our mortgage.
He stole our livestock and our crop.
The court only laughed at our plight
And filled our ears with hollow talk.
You were so bitter, you spat up blood
And the boiling hatred made you ill!
A year ago today you died
And lie buried on this hill.

Tang: *Speaks.* Oh husband – we'd all be better off dead like you! Things grow worse every day! There is no justice!

Ning: Mother! Someone's coming!

Hu enters, as Xu Ying, *the son of a wealthy landlord. With him is Zhou, as* Xu Fu, *the servant.*

Hu: *Recites.*

> And I am Xu Ying, third son
> Of the noble Xu family! *Laughs.*
> I'm here attending ancestral graves
> But the point is to have a bit of fun.
> Oh look! Two juicy peasant girls
> Playing hide-and-seek among the stones.
> Xu Fu, I think it's time
> We joined their little game!

Zhou: As you say, Third Master Xu.

As the women try to flee, Hu intercepts Ning.

Hu: Come, my little bluebird – entertain us with a song!

Tang steps in his way, defiantly.

Hu: Out of the way, bitch! You'll have to wait your turn! I prefer them a little younger.

Tang: I'll thank you to show respect. The girl is my daughter!

Hu: Daughter! Oh wonderful – a combination! Did you hear that, Xu Fu? Invite them *both* to my house!

Tang: Ridiculous! We don't even know you!

Hu: Ha ha! did you hear her, Xu Fu? She doesn't even know me! Ha ha ha! Well, my little delicacy, you will get to know me better. *Taking Ning's hands.* When you become my concubine, you will have new clothes and all the food you want!

Tang: Come, Xiaolan! We are leaving!

He unsheaths his sword.

Hu: Ah, but not so fast.

Tang: Are things so bad in Jiangnan? Women are no longer safe in broad daylight! Help! Father!

Zhou: Don't make so much noise! He won't mistreat you – really! *Confidentially.* He is Third Master Xu – of the Xu family!

Tang: *Horrified.* Third Master Xu! The man who killed my husband! Father, help! Come quickly!

Ning: Grandfather! *Grandfather*!

Chang rushes in, as the peasant Zhao Youshan. *Other* peasants *follow.*

First Peasant: Look – that rotten egg from the Xu family!

Second Peasant: Abusing women again!

First Peasant: It's an outrage!

Second Peasant: Why isn't this monster punished?

Chang: *Defending the women.* Run, my children! I'll stop him! Run while you have a chance!

Tang retreats, but Ning is seized by Zhou. Hu, in a rage, seizes the old man.

Hu: Oh, don't leave, Grandpa. We have something to discuss.

Chang: There is nothing to discuss! Let her go! You hounded my son-in-law to death, you stole our land. Now you insult his widow and daughter! You're a criminal!

Hu: And you are an ignorant old fool! Be still, and I will educate you. Be reasonable, Grandpa, how can you look after these delectable creatures when you don't have a crust to your name? Ha? If you want them to be comfortable, send them to me, and they'll soon be wearing satin and silk.

Chang: Brute!

Hu: What is more, a little co-operation will get *you* a few bowls of rice! Eh?

Chang: *Indignantly.* I am poor, Master Xu, but I am not a pimp! Take your lust and go away! Leave us alone!

Hu: *Sighs.* How ignorant these peasants are! No matter how much I try, they refuse to be educated. Xu Fu! Beat him. Beat this corpse who is too stupid to lie down!

Zhou beats Chang with a pole, as Tang and peasants watch in horror. Hu drags Ming off-stage, and Zhou follows.

First Peasant: The landlords are like a plague.

Second Peasant: Beating people openly!

Tang: What kind of world is this?

First Peasant: There is no law.

Second Peasant: There is no justice.

Chang: *Feebly.* Don't cry, daughter. No time. Hurry to the magistrate. File a complaint against this gangster!

Tang: Why? The court has never helped before!

Chang: There's no other course. We must rescue Xiaolan before it's too late! Run, run – to Magistrate Wang.

Tang: No, father! I must stay and treat your wounds!

First Peasant: Lady, you'd better do what he says.

Second Peasant: We can look after him.

First Peasant: If you're going to do anyting, you have to do it fast!

Tang: Thank you, friends. Thank you!

She rushes out.

Chang and Peasants: *Sing.*

In their tyranny of common folk,
They are worse than the ancient dragon.
Only the law or a mighty force
Will rid us of this sort of brigand!

The peasants assist Chang off, limping. Wu Han appears.

Wu Han: Good. Good work, everyone. The peasants could be a bit more forceful. Second scene!

Music announces second scene.

Yao: The Court of Magistrate Wang.

Bi enters as Magistrate Wang.

Bi: *Recites.*

> Justice is the password to my court,
> For I am a judge of the seventh degree.
> As long as you have plenty of cash,
> Your social rank means nothing to me.
> You don't call Magistrate Wang unfair;
> I'm very well-versed in the laws of old.
> Why, I'd hang my mother if she didn't pay –
> My heart goes soft at the sight of gold!

Peasants enter, shuffling in a line. Tang follows.

Bi: What are all you lot doing here again?

First Peasant: Seeking justice, your honour.

Bi: Well, you found the place! What is your complaint!

First Peasant: I humbly accuse the former Prime Minister's family of seizing my land!

Second Peasant: And I humbly report that Third Master Xu grabbed my cow and pigs!

Bi: *Sighs.* How boring. Ever since I got this promotion, it's all I hear. The Xu family this, the Xu family that! And they're so *unimaginative*! "Stealing land!" A big fuss over a handful of cabbages. *To peasants.* I can't help you without *evidence*! It's your word against the former Prime Minister! And doesn't he hold all the power in this country? You people are so ungrateful! Why don't you try to *get along* with him – like I do? You're too stupid! Go on, get out of my sight!

Peasants scamper out.

Bi: All right, woman, what's your problem? No – let me guess – the Xu family?

Tang: Your Worship, Third Master Xu has beaten my father – a very old man.

Bi: *To attendants.* Well, what did I tell you? I should be an astrologer.

Tang: And he's kidnapped my daughter!

Bi: Really? Well, this is more interesting. Messenger, summon Third Master Xu from Suziou, to hear this charge against him. *To Tang.* Now, what's this about your daughter? Are you sure it's not just a simple – infatuation?

Tang: I tell you he abducted her!

Bi: But you have some witnesses?

Tang: Several peasants! They stayed behind to tend my father, or they would be here now!

Bi: Oho – now it begins to smell! No evidence. No witnesses. Where *is* this alleged "father?"

Tang: He was hurt so badly, he can't move!

Bi: How convenient. You think I don't know all your tricks? I used to be a peasant, too, you know! If he won't come and show his injuries, how can I believe you? This has all the earmarks of malice, slander and blackmail!

Tang: Your Worship, if you are honest, investigate my complaint.

Bi: What? "*If* I'm *honest*?" The nerve! You bring these witnesses, and you'll get so much justice your head will buzz! Go on. Hop it!

Tang goes out weeping.

Bi: Hmmm. Kidnapping – and beating! No, no – not the *Xus*. But still – could be lucrative. No point in stirring up the former Prime Minister but – if she has witnesses, we'll have to investigate . . . *Paces about.* I know. I'll ask Prefect Li for his advice! He'll know what to do. *Turns at the exit and sings.*

Day by day, rebellious people rock the boat.
It's not easy for a magistrate to stay afloat!

He goes out. Music.

Yao: Magistrate Wang's court. The next day!

Bi: *Recites.*

No longer must I scavenge from the poor;
Today my fortune has been made.
The Xu family has sent buckets of money,
Enough to buy Wang a belt of jade.
And hundreds of people will flock to court
To hear my words of wisdom said!

Hu and Zhou enter.

Hu: Who would have expected the bitch to *complain*? With *me* looking after her daughter! Did you give the magistrate three hundred pieces of gold?

Zhou: Yes, Third Master Xu.

Hu: And two hundred more for Prefect Li?

Zhou: Yes, Third Master Xu.

Hu: Well, this stooge knows who fills *his* rice bowl. He'll take care of peasants who don't know their place. You memorized the story?

Zhou: Yes, Third Master Xu.

Bi: Summon the peasants in the case of Hong Alan's complaint against Third Master Xu.

Drum sounds. Tang, Chang and Peasants enter.

Peasants: Our humble respects to Your Worship.

Bi: Enough! Servility cannot sway my judgement! Well, what a miserable gang of vermin. I hope you understand the seriousness of your complaint. This Master Xu –

Bi and Hu smile and nod at each other.

Bi: – whom you have accused of misdeeds – is the son of the beloved Xu Jieh, formerly Prime Minister of the Empire, and a friend of the Emperor himself!

The peasants react.

Bi: So tell only the facts. One lie and you are in deep trouble. Where is Hong Alan?

Tang: Here.

Bi: Have you brought your witnesses today?

First Peasant: Here we are.

Second Peasant: It happened right in front of us!

Bi: And the so-called beaten father? Where is he?

Chang: Here!

Bi: Well – where are the injuries? I note that you can walk.

Chang: *Points.* All over my body!

Bi: Any other witnesses?

Second Peasant: It happened right in front of our eyes!

Bi: Oh, all right. Remove your shirt.

Chang lifts his shirt. There are red welts over his body.

Bi: Eh? *To peasants.* The brass of you people! His body is hardly even marked! Bring the cane and give him a *real* beating!

Chang: Your honour, I beg you – exam carefully! I can *feel* these cuts and bruises!

First Peasant: This man took a frightful beating, sir! We saw it with our own humble eyes!

Second Peasant: From that slave there! If we're lying, you can beat us too!

Bi: That is possible! Nothing but your word against Master Xu's – yet the whole gang sticks to their story!

Chang puts his battered body right under Bi's nose.

Bi: Whew! Well – I do see a few cuts – probably self-inflicted, or from a fall. But definitely *not* evidence of a beating. I call Xu Ying to testify.

Hu: The noble Xu family sends their deepest respects to Your Worship.

Bi: *Bowing and scraping.* No need to stand on ceremony, Sir. Now – these people accuse you of kidnapping a girl, and beating this old man. Is there is any truth to the accusations?

Hu: I am a member of the former Prime Minister's household! I am devoted to studying great scholars of philosophy! Why would I be involved in that nonsense?

Bi: A needless question, Sir!

Hu: May I ask *when* this beating is alleged to have occurred?

Bi gestures at Tang to speak.

Tang: During Chingming Festival!

Hu: Chingming Festival? Let me see, where was I? Oh, yes – I was at the house of Scholar Duan in Suzhou, discussing classics.

Bi: You have a witness, I think?

Hu: My personal servant, Xu Fu, was with me.

Bi: Xu Fu! Tell us what your master did on that day.

Zhou: *Mechanically.* I report to Your Worship that Master Xu was studying at the home of Scholar Duan, and never left Suzhou. I was with him the whole time.

Bi: So! This man must have a double, whom you saw at the mountainside, kidnapping and beating people! Or is this another false accusation against the Xu family?

Tang: *Bravely.* They are lying, Your Honour!

Bi: What? *Lying*? I warn you, creature – you can be thrashed, as well! Is that your only defence? Can't you even beg for mercy?

Music for "Mercy." Tang and Chang sing.

Tang: Mercy, Your Honour! Mercy, please!
We are poor farmers who need help.

Chang: Two years ago we lost our land
To this Master Xu himself.

Tang: He made up a cheating contract
Which drove my husband wild.

Chang: The boy died of a brain-stroke,
Leaving this widow and child!

Chang and Tang:

The Xus demanded our taxes!
We were bond slaves on our land!
One blow followed another –
Will the law punish us again?
Where is the magistrate's conscience?
Where are the ancient principles of justice?

Bi: *Recites.*

What evil creatures you all are!
You accuse this noble gentleman

Not only of beating up strangers,
But also of stealing your land!
Some "ancient principle of justice!"
You're a disgrace to the human race!
Remove this scoundrel from my sight
And beat him till he learns his place!

Chang: I warn you, magistrate. You are not above the law! We'll report you!

First Peasant: Shhh! Take it easy, comrade!

Bi: *Amused.* And who will you report to, peasant?

Second Peasant: Be quiet, Uncle Zhao! You'll make it worse!

Chang: I'll go to the capital, to the prefect in Suzhou! *Sings.*

When old men are treated like dogs,
Even heaven must be offended.
My tortured body shall be avenged,
My kidnapped girl defended.

Your office does not tender justice,
but sells it for the highest fee!

First Peasant: Uncle Zhao, *be quiet*!

Chang: We will fight corrupt officials
Until the people's law is free!

Bi: Monster! Snake! *Sings*:

This man confesses to sedition!
Such self-destruction is insane.
Take him out and treat him to

Eighty strokes of bamboo cane!

Zhou and attendants remove Chang, and he is beaten, off-stage. Bi serves tea to Hu.

Bi: A bowl of tea?

Hu: Thank you. A busy day today?

Bi: Not bad. Just this case, and a few petty thefts.

Hu: We must deal severely with these crimes. The whole country suffers.

Zhou re-enters, apprehensive.

Zhou: I regret to report, Your Worship – but the plaintiff suddenly died in the midst of his punishment.

Bi: Oh dear.

Hu: Tsk, tsk, tsk.

Tang suddenly stands and shouts.

Tang: Murders! *You* are the criminals! And to your faces I swear revenge!

Bi: Stop her mouth! Remove her from the court! And have the old beggar's carcass taken out and buried!

The peasants and attendants go out with Tang.

Hu: Well, you are busy, Magistrate. And I have many things to attend to.

Bi: Good day, Master Xu. It's been a pleasure to serve you.

Hu goes out, with Zhou.

Bi: Ai-ya! I'm getting careless. The old fool should have been able to take a few strokes of the cane. *Pacing.* Aa, no need to worry. Such things happen all the time in Jiangnan. Even the Emperor must be severe. It is the nature of government. Who can be perfect all the time?

Yao: An urgent despatch from Suzhou.

Bi reads the letter.

Bi: A curse on us all! A new governor!

Yao: What's wrong? A tyrant?

Bi: Worse! An honest official! Hai Rui, the former adviser to the emperor. He's just been appointed Governor of Jiangnan! I must confer with the prefect again. . . .

There is a sudden eruption of noise, banging and shouting off-stage, at the main door. All action stops.

Chang: *Running in.* It's the Red Guards!

Li: No! It can't be!

Chang: Come on! Let's get out of here!

Tang: Wait, don't panic!

Bi: They're only students! They're serving the revolution – !

Chang: They've got guns!

Li: Go back! We have to maintain order!

Feng Bao-da and Lin Hulan burst into the theatre, shouting and waving copies of Mao's Quotations. *They are in quasi-military dress.*

Feng: Death to revisionists!

Lin: Where is the traitor Wu Han?

Ning: It's him! The one who chased me!

Feng: Death to the capitalist-roaders!

Lin: Give us the renegade Wu Han!

The cast is milling about on stage, surrounding Wu Han.

Feng: Smash the fascist clique!

Feng pulls a gun from his belt and points it at the crowd.

Lin: Where is Wu Han?

Feng: *We want Wu Han*!

The actors draw away from the pointed pistol. Wu Han faces the Guards alone as the lights begin to fade. Zhou is standing at one side with a red Mao book.

Zhou: *Reading, in wonder.* "Power comes from the barrel of a gun!"

Blackout on tableau.

End of Act One

Act Two

The lights come up on a new tableau: Wu Han is seated in the centre of the group, faced by Lin Hulan and Feng Baoda, the two Red Guards. Zhou is missing. Yao is at the edge of the group, repairing an electrical fixture.

Lin: This is the accusation! The renegade scholar and author Wu Han has been stirring up bad elements in the university. We have been sent to rectify him, and call on the assistance of all true revolutionaries!

Li: Who sent you?

Feng: Chairman Mao!

Lin: As the revolutionary vanguard, Red Guards from all over China must preserve the purity of Mao Zedong Thought.

Feng: We are the storm troops of the Cultural Revolution! We'll smash this gangster into the dirt!

Lin: Under the guidance of Lin Biao, Chairman Mao's closest comrade, we have struggled in Great Debates for three days. Now we have been ordered to root out class enemies and traitors like this – *points to Wu Han* – and make him confess his crimes against the people.

Li: And who are you?

Lin: I am Lin Hulan, leader of Red Flag brigade, and this is Feng Baoda, a comrade from Fu Dan University in Shanghai.

Feng: Who are *you*, comrade?

Li: I am Li Chen, party secretary of the Central Academy of Drama. A Communist for twenty-five years!

Lin: You think that will protect you?

Feng: The party in Beijing is rotten with bourgeois elements!

Lin: This – *criminal* was first identified six months ago by our comrades in Shanghai – but still he is protected by right-wing elements in Beijing!

Feng: Now we'll smash the whole gang!

The group reacts, murmuring with apprehension.

Feng: And if you don't join us, we'll bring in reinforcements and struggle you all!

Lin: The workers will arise spontaneously against such puppets of the ruling class!

Li : *To Wu Han.* I'm going for the army! They'll settle this.

Wu Han: No no. They want to have a struggle session. Let it proceed. We will have a struggle of intellects.

Feng: You! *To Bi.* How did this enemy of the people spread his poison within the academy?

Bi: *Uncertainly.* Well, he is – the author. A professor.

Feng: He is a fascist! An agent of the Kuomintang!

Bi: Oh . . .

Lin: This whole academy needs instruction in the principles of the

Great Proletarian Cultural Revolution. Which is the student you first saw?

Feng: Her!

He points at Ning.

Lin: Comrade student. How did you become involved in this traitorous plot?

Ning: It is not a plot. It is a revolutionary drama, and I am proud to be in it.

Bi: I personally am more skeptical, comrade – but I am only a student. What can we do?

Feng: You can smash the conspiracy of reactionary scholars! It is your duty as a student! What is this? A den of reactionaries?

Chang: No, no! We are very progressive! As professional actors, we sometimes have to do unpleasant work!

Tang: We are working under the authority of the Cultural Group of the City Committee. We've debated the politics of this play several times, and we believe it is revolutionary art –

Lin: You do not decide these things!

Li: Oh? Who does?

Feng: The left vanguard! The masses!

Tang: I am sorry, comrade, to contradict, but I was an actor in the People's Liberation Army during the war. I've been in touch with the masses.

Feng: The Red Guards are the true left. All over China, red brigades are seizing universities, theatres, and other dens of reactionary thought!

Lin: Mark our words, comrades. The Cultural Revolution we're leading for Chairman Mao will conclude with an international uprising of revolutionary youth!

Feng: Armed with Mao Zedong Thought, we will smash the palaces of decadent authority around the world! In Asia, in Europe! Even America!

Bi: Long live Chairman Mao.

Feng, Chang and Lin: Long live Chairman Mao!

Wu Han: This has nothing to do with the drama!

Lin: We will deal with your lies in good time, *Mister* Professor. First, the masses must be prepared.

Hu: *We* are the masses?

Feng: Shut up!

Lin: *Wielding the little Red Book.* We are informed that the so-called ideas in this drama are anti-Marxist.

Wu Han: Do you know what they are? Have you even read the play?

Lin: I am no ignorant lackey of your bourgeois university, Mister Professor! I have read *and* analyzed this play!

Wu Han: Oh?

Lin: You are surprised?

Wu Han: Moderately.

Lin: This is not only an obsolete form – the Kunchu Opera – but the ideas stink of Confucius.

Wu Han: That was once considered a compliment.

Feng: Only Jiang Qing's revolutionary operas will be allowed in the New China!

Lin: In your decadent plot, the peasants do not rise in struggle against the landlords, but pray for some so-called "good official" to deliver them. Correct?

Wu Han: Not at all. They are seeking justice. Is that reactionary?

Feng: We will ask the questions!

Lin: Then this so-called hero of the ruling classes, Hai Rui, suddenly dispenses justice in the feudal society? Am I right?

Wu Han: I state only that Hai Rui was a man who refused to submit to tyranny. And that people of any age, feudal or modern, can learn from his example. It does not matter which class he came from.

Feng: I am writing this down!

Lin: In your opinion, Professor, what will the Chinese proletariat learn from your so-called story?

Wu Han: That is a good question, comrade. The central question.

Lin: Indeed? We await your instruction.

Wu Han: It is about history. Do you believe that people can learn from history?

Lin: We're not here to find out what we think! It's to discover what *you* think.

Wu Han: In the West, it is said, "Those who do not learn from history are doomed to repeat it."

Feng: *Writing*. Quoting Western imperialist dogma!

Lin: And what do we learn from your "cycles of history," Mister Professor?

Wu Han: Whatever is there.

Feng: *Threatening*. I'll put a stop to your fascist equivocating!

Lin: No, Feng! Group mass criticism.

Tang: Comrades, the play contains several complex political questions . . .

Hu: It does not! It's just a melodrama; nothing to do with politics at all. It's for entertaining people! What's wrong with that?

Lin: "Entertainment" is a capitalist idea, comrade. *Quoting from book*. "All art is political." That is why we destroy the old forms of theatre. There is no difference between cultural and political struggle. Art must serve the revolution!

Wu Han: In my opinion, *Hai Rui's Dismissal* serves the revolution!

Lin: Then you admit that it is political!

Wu Han: Of course. *Pointing to the book*. "All art has political intent." Our only disagreement is in what serves the great Chinese revolution.

Lin: Your brazenness is impressive, Mister Professor. Do elaborate for us, and for these cultural workers you've duped into performing.

Wu Han: You have heard of "The Hundred Flowers" movement?

Feng: The anti-rightist campaign of 1957.

Wu Han: That came later. "The Hundred Flowers" was a slogan for free-expression.

Hu: *Sardonically.* "Let a hundred flowers bloom. Let a hundred schools of thought contend."

Li: When people began to criticize the leadership, they were denounced and sent to labour camps. The very thing being criticized!

Wu Han: There were many suicides. Suddenly our intellectuals and writers had become bigger enemies than the landlords!

Feng: They were puppets of the counter-revolution!

Wu Han: They criticized. Just as the Red Guards criticize today. Is that counter-revolutionary?

Lin: So you *defend* those who criticize our leaders?

Wu Han: Of course. When revolutionaries come to office and abuse their power, what kind of revolution is that? The old forms of oppression appear again. True revolutionaries are *critics* of power, not seekers of power. Hai Rui was such a man.

Lin: Then revolution itself is a contradiction?

Wu Han: You don't believe in "contradictions" comrades?

Lin: Don't play your clever semantic tricks with us, *professor*. We are not fools!

Wu Han: Contradictions are the essence of the dialectical process. And they are rarely resolved in political debate. That is what art is for. And scholarship.

Feng: Scholars are criminals! They've stolen the people's education! *We* will liberate the universities from the scholars!

Lin: Don't be so easily led from the topic. Let us stick to the play.

Feng: Right! Why aren't you criticizing this gangster?

Ning: On what grounds should we criticize him, comrades?

Tang: We've studied all these charges before.

Li: None of them has any weight.

Lin: All right. We charge this drama with betraying the Chinese Revolution by – *consulting a paper* – "glorifying ghosts and monsters from the past." Plays about feudal times are irrelevant and dangerous in the new China.

Feng: Lin Biao told us, "Smash the four olds! Old ideas, old culture, old customs, and old habits!" They must be destroyed for a revolutionary society to flourish.

Wu Han: Destroy all culture from the past? All art? And literature?

Lin: Everything which does not promote socialism. In the new

China, culture is for the workers and peasants. If the left vanguard does not control art and culture, the revolution will fail.

Li: But who represents the left vanguard?

Feng: We do! The Red Guards are more left than *anyone*!

Lin: *Mister* Professor – it is true this play is set in the feudal period?

Wu Han: The Ming dynasty. Sixteenth century.

Lin: *Reading from the Red Book.* So. Chairman Mao says, "Copying from the ancients is the most sterile dogmatism in literature and art."

Wu Han: I agree. But also remember, *pointing to the book, quoting from memory*, "We must take over the rich legacy and traditions handed down from past ages."

Feng: That is a direct contradiction!

Wu Han: Yes, even the Chairman enjoys contradictions. He too is an historian.

Lin: The people are not interested in your theories! Feudal landlords and emperors have all been liquidated. No one wants to hear about them any longer!

Ning: That's not true! Lots of people are interested. Anyway, it's a modern play *about* ancient times!

Feng: What are you, a lackey of this turtle?

Bi: Pay no attention. She's only a first-year student.

Ning: I am from a peasant family, so I know what the people like!

Lin: Comrade, you have a lot to learn. Join us in our struggle against the tyranny of old traditions.

Feng: And old men!

Bi: Right. Together we can cut out the rotten feudal past!

Wu Han: But if the past was evil, then our ancestors were evil, and we'd all be descendants of evil men! No, I think not. Ours is a great history! There were many great men before liberation.

Feng: Name one!

Wu Han: Well – Hai Rui.

Tang: Professor, *please*.

Lin: *Glaring*. This brings us to the next charge. *Consulting book*. You have "allowed emperors, generals, prime ministers and scholars to dominate the stage!" I believe your hero is a member of the ruling class?

Feng: He's a disgusting *official*! A puppet of the emperor.

Chang: I knew they'd throw that at us!

Tang: But he is a revolutionary figure!

Bi: *I* never agreed to that.

Lin: You have debated this before?

Hu: A hundred times.

Feng: *Incredulous.* And you didn't stop this crap?

Tang: The play is about a struggle between Hai Rui and the ruling class.

Li: A struggle before the "left" views of Hai Rui and the right faction of the grasping officials. Clear-cut!

Lin: Nonsense! You are missing the point. How can we ever progress, if people cling to values from the old China?

Ning: Is justice ancient history? Are you going to abolish justice?

Bi: Listen to her. Twittering about "justice!"

Wu Han: You would destroy our old world to build the new? Level *everything*?

Feng: Smash it all!

Wu Han: What's the point in tearing down the *symbols* of the past? They are superficial. The changes must be *inside*, comrades. It is corruption and privilege we must smash. The oppression of the people. We cannot change the fact that this occurred.

Lin: How reasonable you make it sound! But who decides what is corrupt and what is valuable – Mister Professor? The scholars – or we the people?

Li: You are not people! You are a gang of bullies!

Feng: Don't you understand *anything*, renegade? Don't you know why Chairman Mao picked us to lead the glorious Cultural Revolution? Society is rotten! And the function of the young is like a fresh living cell in the human body. We must drive out the old and the rotten! Eliminate them! If a society is filled with rot, it will sicken and die! That is why you and your Confucian ideas about "justice" are doomed – Professor!

Bi: Exactly. Get rid of the scholars!

Ning: Coward. Turncoat!

Lin: What about the rest of you?

Chang: We've learned our lesson. We'll be much more vigilant from now on.

Feng: You! *Pointing suddenly to Yao.* You, actor!

Yao: *Calmly.* I'm not an actor. I'm a worker.

Feng: Fine! A worker. What do *you* think of this garbage!

Yao: What do I think? I'll tell you, comrade. I don't think. I'm not an intellectual. I don't get paid to think!

Feng: Don't evade me!

He pulls out his gun.

Lin: No! Feng! Be patient.

Ning: This is ridiculous. Nobody will criticize Professor Wu. Why don't you go and write posters or something?

Bi: An ignorant girl from the countryside. Knows nothing about politics.

Ning: As much as you! The brat of a party official – spying on people for your VIP father.

Feng: What? A black element?

Bi: No! She's – lying. Well, exaggerating.

Lin: Your father is a high-level cadre?

Bi: Yes – but I – I belong to a Red Guard brigade in the history department. I'm a radical!

Wu Han: You'd be advised to keep your mouth shut, Bi.

Feng: *To Bi.* Stand with him! You'll be struggled, too.

Li: How long do we have to put up with this?

Tang: Comrades, we are *all* dedicated to the revolution. Surely this can be discussed without –

Hu: Is this a struggle session?

Ning: We keep going in circles.

Feng: The struggle will go on until this renegade confesses his crimes!

Li: Like hell it will! I'm getting the soldiers!

Feng. Stand back!

Tang: Comrades, there must be authority! Chaos won't get us anywhere.

Li: Stand aside! These idiots will be taught a lesson!

Feng: I warn you!

The argument grows into a shoving match, centres around Feng and Li. Angry shouts are leading to a brawl. Lin suddenly seizes Feng's gun, and fires it into the air. She is left standing in the centre, trembling with anger.

Lin: The struggle will proceed! We'll criticize his crimes till he confesses!

Zhou suddenly staggers in, with a bag full of pastries.

Zhou What is it? Another revolution?

Lin: What?

Feng: Who is he?

Wu Han: The sweeper. He's harmless.

Lin: Join us, comrade sweeper. We need your testimony in this struggle session.

Zhou: *Approaching.* Well, isn't Uncle Zhou an important man today! Who are you?

Feng: The Red Flag detachment of Red Guards. We are making revolution. And you?

Zhou: Zhou Suchen of the Tiger Division of the Eighth Route Army, and I'm just bringing these people some lunch.

There is some laughter, breaking the tension. He passes out baozi *rolls to the actors. They crowd around.*

Zhou All right, take it easy!

Wu Han: Do you have any for our guests, Uncle Zhou?

Zhou: *With contempt.* Them? *Looks closely.* They're intellectuals. Let them eat words!

Chang: Be careful!

Feng: Who is this old monkey?

Ning: Just a harmless old man. Our janitor.

Zhou offers some to the two Guards. After a brief hesitation, they take one each and gobble them down, clearly famished.

Zhou: Hungry as jackals!

Tang: Have you had nothing to eat?

Lin: Not much – we're like the Red Army – "rely on the people to provide!"

Tang: All of you? Where do you sleep?

Feng: In the streets. Sometimes factories. Wherever we forge solidarity with the workers.

Lin: Comrade Zhou, have you seen this drama?

Zhou: Seen it? I'm in it!

Feng: What!

Zhou: After all those years – an actor at last. Watch me *grovel*!

He gestures.

Lin: Come here. Does this play – serve the Revolution?

Zhou: I don't understand the question, Comrade Guard. Which

Revolution?

Feng: Ridiculous. His brains are addled.

Lin: *Sharply.* You need more patience, Comrade Feng. *To Zhou, carefully.* Does this drama present feudal ideas or not? As a worker, you can be frank.

Zhou: Well, I – never thought about that. Why don't you just watch us and decide for yourself?

Lin: I value your opinion, even above the others.

Zhou: *Gesturing "you see" to others.* Well, if you ask me, it's a bit melodramatic – but feudal? Didn't we get rid of all that in '49? *Uncertain.* No, perhaps not. . . .

Feng: He doesn't know anything! None of them do! Except him! [Wu Han].

Lin: I now perceive the correct course of action. We will allow the rehearsal to proceed!

Feng: What?

General reaction.

Lin: Our struggle will succeed only when these workers understand the conspiracy they have been lured into. They must study the play as it unfolds.

Feng: No! *Our* orders were to smash the play and seize the renegade!

Lin: We can't retreat from struggle for the minds of the masses, Feng. That admits his power.

Feng: We had a specific task!

Lin: First we will reveal the sinister poison of the drama to these people. Do you agree, Mister Professor?

Wu Han: I will allow the drama to speak for me. That is my form of struggle. What do you say, Comrade Tang?

Tang: Well, I – if you think –

Feng: You're playing into his hands.

Chang: *Disbelieving.* You mean, we're *proceeding*?

Bi: I refuse to take part!

Lin: Everyone will take part!

Wu Han: Aaa. In fact – we are rather short-handed today. Perhaps the Red Guards could read some lines? Forge solidarity with the workers?

Hu: Madness!

Lin: You can joke, Professor, but I warn you that I've performed in revolutionary operas. I was *chosen* for this mission.

Wu Han: Excellent. What do you think, Tianmei? Where can we employ these volunteers?

Chang: We'll be executed for sure!

Tang: They could be court officials. Or peasants. Do you have more scripts, Yao?

Wu Han: Good idea. We have to fill out the court scenes.

Feng: I won't do it!

Lin: "Seeing once is worth a hundred descriptions." We must accept this challenge – or fail. Here's a script! Don't be afraid – I'll take responsibility.

Feng: You are not my superior!

Lin: *Indicating her paper.* I hold the charge-sheet!

For a moment, Feng is undecided. Then he takes a script.

Feng: *Examining a script.* But I won't be a black element. I will only play a revolutionary!

Wu Han: Pick your own role. Anything you like.

Chang: He can have my parts!

Hu: I hope the Academy doesn't hear about this. We'll never live it down.

Tang: Just stand where Yao shows you and read the lines as marked.

Wu Han: All set?

Yao: Places, everyone.

Lin: Now remember – you have heard the charges. You must *think* about them, as you analyze the play.

Yao: Musicians in the pit? We begin with Hai Hui's entrance!

Music.

Lin: The pavilion at the gates of Suzhou! One month later.

Bi and Chang enter, waving fans.

Chang: Well, where is this new Governor? Another useless wait!

Bi: He will soon be here, Prefect Li. The runners say he left Nanjing yesterday, riding in this direction.

Chang: Ridiculous! Everyone's in a panic. The landlords are hiding their red robes! And the manager of the silk factory has reduced the slaves on his sedan chair from eight to four. Afraid of a minor official!

Bi: Everyone says he is incorruptible! That could wreck everything. Well, you served in the capital! You must have known him.

Chang: *Recites.*

This Hai Rui was so stiff-necked
that he earned the name "Unyielding."
He even criticized Emperor Jia Jing!
Accused him of being unfeeling.
He said the Emperor's lust for power
Was a waste of money and time
When he could be helping the people
By relieving famine and crime.
Oh, the emperor flew into a rage.
He condemned Hai Rui to his death!
And the fool refused to give in.
He prepared to draw his last breath.

Bi: Good heavens!

Chang: – The emperor finally relented,
After Hai Rui spent months in jail.
And now – he's sent here as governor.
He's never been known to fail.

Bi: *Nervously.* I hope we've covered our tracks!

Chang: *Irritably.* This heat! Let us wait inside the gate. We can get some wine!

They move inside the gate. Wu Han enters as Hai Rui, *with Ning as Hai Rui's wife,* Wang Shih.

Ning: Ah, husband, it is so hot I am wilting! Can we stop and rest for a moment?

Wu Han: We are nearly there. Here is Suzhou city gate. We can rest in this pavilion, out of the sun.

Ning: Where are the servants, dear husband?

Wu Han: I sent them on ahead. I want to arrive as inconspicuously as possible.

Tang enters, weeping.

Feng: Wait a minute! *Stop everything*!

Tang: What is it?

Feng: Who are these stupid court officials, anyway? That's exactly what's been banned!

Bi: That's what I was trying to say!

Feng: *Disgusting*! Monsters from the past!

Wu Han: That is exactly the point. They were realities in the pre-revolutionary past!

Feng: Keep your bourgeois theories to yourself. I say, remove them.

Lin: Don't be ignorant, Feng. Even revolutionary operas need villains. What concerns me more is *this* creature. *Indicating Ning.* I suppose she is the heroine.

Tang: In a sense.

Lin: Does she have to be a silly little wife with bound feet?

Wu Han: That's the way it was. We can't change history.

Lin: But if Hai Rui was so "progressive," why would he marry such a simpering noodle?

Ning: She is a typical devoted wife. It *was* before Liberation, after all.

Lin: *Making a note.* It will be changed. No more bound feet on stage.

Wu Han: The play is set in the sixteenth century!

Feng: We live in the twentieth century!

Wu Han: I can't change that!

Tang: Professor Wu, they have a point. I confess she has always bothered me a bit, too.

Wu Han: Oh, Tianmei – don't you start . . .

Lin: Bound feet are feudal and obscene!

Bi: So are corrupt officials and nobles! Down with ghosts and emperors.

Ning: What are you complaining about? Are you so afraid of your middle class background you're trying to out-Red the Red Guards?

Yao: It's ten-thirty, Director!

Tang: *Claps her hands.* All right, we're straying from the point. Bound feet! In or out?

Wu Han consults his script, hesitates.

Ning: It's probably my performance. I'll try to make her more contemporary.

Lin: The fault is in the writing, not the playing.

Wu Han: She can walk with unbound feet, if that will help.

Yao: From the top of the scene, then?

Lin: Proceed.

Wu Han: Hong Alan's entrance.

Music repeats. Tang enters, crying. A blind peasant Story-teller, *read by Yao, enters opposite.*

Yao: Curse upon this heat! Why are you crying, woman? Has someone harmed you?

Tang: *Sings.*

My heart is torn with grief and hate –
I beg heaven to hear my cry!
I call a curse upon this land
That condemned an honest man to die!
Is there hope in a world

Where wrong cannot be told from right?
Where men of the law conspire to hold
A woman's daughter from her sight?
My heart is torn with grief and hate. . . .

Yao: The usual story. It's awful! What can you do?

Tang: I'm looking for the Governor's yamen, to make a complaint. He is a new official, and rumoured to be honest. A reformer.

Yao: Ha! Our system eats up reformers like bean-shoots! If you want change, you'd better change the system!

Tang: One lone woman? Change the system? Good sir, where is the Governor's yamen?

Wu Han: Why do you want to speak to the Governor?

Tang: My father was murdered by the gentry in Huating County!

Wu Han: Murdered? Report this to your local Magistrate. The Governor only deals with higher cases.

Tang: Oh sir, you must be a stranger – the Magistrate ordered the execution! He said we were slandering the landlords.

Yao: Yes, yes, same old story.

Wu Han: No witnesses?

Tang: Many. But the Magistrate would only believe Xu Ying's bond slave!

Wu Han: Xu Ying? Son of the former Prime Minister?

Tang: Yes.

Yao: That devil! He's notorious for his extortion and brutality!

Wu Han: Then why isn't he stopped? Surely if this woman has witnesses –

Yao: Ha ha. *Recites with clappers.*

Sir, you jabber away like an ignorant fool.
In Jiangnan, the laws are for the wealthy.
If witnesses began to tell what they saw –
Their lives wouldn't be so healthy.

Wu Han: But all it takes is one individual to resist. To act according to the truth.

Yao: That individual would be liquidated! Only the landlord class is believed. The peasants are liars by definition.

Wu Han: Then perhaps the new Governor is corrupt, too.

Yao: My opinion, precisely.

Tang: I have nowhere else to turn!

Wu Han: Then petition him, woman. Sometimes an official, if he hears the people, can make great changes!

Musical fanfare, off. Bi and Chang rush in through the gate. Tang flees at the sight of them.

Tang: It's them!

Chang: The official announcement!

Bi: Hai Rui has arrived!

Chang: Hail to the new Governor!

Bi: Hail to Governor Hai!

They run into Yao and Wu Han, knocking them aside.

Bi: You clumsy old fool!

Chang Watch where you're going!

Bi and Chang: *Together, roaring.* Beat them!

They go off, shouting "Hail to Governor Hai Rui!"

Music begins for Hai-Wang duet.

Wu Han: *Sings.*

> These petty officials put on airs
> And treat the people like slaves!
> Now Governor Hai Rui will defend the people
> And sweep away these knaves.
> Protect the meek and crush the sinister –
> Even if we offend the former Prime Minister!

Ning: *Re-enters singing.*

> In the streets and alleys of Suzhou
> They all say he's come from heaven.
> They expect he'll perform miracles,
> Forgetting that he's just a man.
> When I think of what he's suffered
> In taking a strict moral line –
> Well, bravery's to be admired
> But survival is the main ideal of mine!

Speaking. My lord, people say the former Prime Minister is the leader of the Jiangnan gentry! A move against them could cost you your head.

Wu Han: What are you saying, Wang Shih? You want me to bow to them, because they hold the reins of power? You don't know me very well.

Ning: *Sighs.* I know you too well, and I fear your notions of justice will make you a martyr. I prefer a husband. If you could only wait a while before taking up each cause – I am sure you would obtain better results.

Wu Han: *Sings.*

What sort of breeze blows past her ears
To make her speak this way?
Conflict only steels my will.
My course shall never be swayed!

Ning: *Sings.*

Lord Hai, for over thirty years,
You served the Emperor well.
But if you criticize the Xus,
We find ourselves in hell!
The gentry must defend their privilege,
And their power remains immense.
The retribution of their wrath
Makes wisdom look like nonsense.

Wu Han: Silence, Wang Shih! My task is clear! *Sings.*

If Hai Rui bent the imperial law
To gain privilege for himself,

How could he face the people?
Where would they turn for help?
No, my wife – the law must stand;
Through me is justice spoken.
The poor and friendless shall prevail,
The tyrants shall be broken!

Ning: *Sings.*

My lord, I yield to your wisdom,
Though I see a dismal future now.

Wu Han: *Sings.*

If I am fated to lose this struggle
We will be exiled anyhow.
And we may finally find a life of peace
In the blue mountains of Qiung-zhao.

Ning: *Sings.*

In the blue mountains of Qiung-zhao!

Wu Han: *Tenderly.* Come, my dear. Time to begin the task. Have no fear – the laws of history are on our side.

They exit.

Lin: The mansion of the former Prime Minister! One week later.

Li enters as Xu Jie.

Li: *Sings.*

I, Xu Jie, for twenty years
Held power of the highest in state.

My name was known throughout the land
When I retired to my country estate.
Now my old friend, Hai Rui, "Unyielding,"
Has come to our place.
It's been years since I heard his voice
And looked on his virtuous face.
The older he grows, the wiser.
He may inspire our restless youth.
And he and I can wile away hours
Debating the meaning of truth.

Zhou: Lord Xu, your slave begs to inform that the new Governor has come from Suzhou to pay his respects.

Li: At last! Well, show him in, show him in! And bring us some tea.

Zhou goes out. Wu Han enters.

Wu Han: Prime Minister Xu!

Li: Lord Hai Rui!

They bow.

Li: And how are you, "Unyielding?"

Wu Han: *Laughing.* Well – stiff as ever, as you can see. Please forgive my delay in calling. My duties have kept me in Suzhou.

Li: Nonsense. I am growing old and feeble, or I would have gone to see you myself.

They sit down. Zhou serves tea.

Wu Han: But you look as healthy as ever!

Li: Well, I still have my teeth, so I can eat meat! Has your wife come with you?

Wu Han: She sends her regards.

Li: I shall ask my two youngest wives to call on her.

Wu Han: Very kind of you.

Li: We are honoured by your visit, Lord Hai. Was there something you wished to discuss?

Wu Han: I came to pay my respects and – I would like your advice on a vexing question.

Li: My life's experience is at your service.

Wu Han: You are a respected elder in Jiangnan, and no doubt have many good ideas to improve the quality of government.

Li: Ha, ha. You are always direct, old friend, but also diplomatic. And since you ask, I will be frank. *Recites.*

> Jiangnan people are very crafty,
> And always try to flout the laws.
> But justice is blind and serves the state.
> It must be obeyed despite its flaws.
> The peasants here lack social fibre
> And rebel against the regulations.
> To be governor will take great courage,
> To apply the law without reservation.

Wu Han: I can apply the law, my lord – though I don't agree that it is blind. In fact, a just official must constantly search into the darker corners, where rot begins to appear. *Pause.* Is there a possibility the gentry here is exploiting the law?

Li: Good heavens! Has someone told you this? Dismiss it from your mind! This is the Ming Empire! We have overcome such barbarity. But I will tell you something, Lord Hai. If you ever hear reports of the gentry abusing its power – just tell me. I will deal with it personally.

Wu Han: Thank you. I will remember. There is one final thing.

Li: Yes?

Wu Han: A peasant woman from Hauting County has accused someone in your household of serious crimes: seizing land, kidnapping a girl, and having an old man beaten to death. In your learned opinion – how should I handle this?

Li: *Shocked.* What is this? Who has been accused?

Wu Han: Third Master Xu Ying.

Li: I see. Well – I'm afraid this is another example of the peasants' devious ways, Lord Hai. All of our land was legally purchased, you see. And as for my son – well he's a bit headstrong, but he's not an utter fool! Kidnapping? Beating people? The days of the Mongols are over. You have to take such slander with a grain of salt.

Wu Han: There is no truth to the complaint?

Li: Of course not.

Wu Han: What if it were proven?

Li: Impossible. Barely one chance in a thousand!

Wu Han: But if it were the one in a thousand?

Li: Well. If there were proof – you should treat it as demanded by the law.

Wu Han: Good! Good! "As demanded by the law." Well said, Prime Minister. Spoken with integrity. I must return to the capital now. Thank you for your advice.

Li: But, Lord Hai – surely you won't –

Wu Han: Yes?

Li: Won't – won't leave us so soon?

Wu Han: I regret that duty calls. Good-bye.

Li: Good-bye.

They bow formally. Wu Han goes out.

Li: Servant! Summon Third Master Xu!

Zhou: *Off.* Calling Third Master Xu!

Li: Ai-ya! Like an earthquake! Just like the old Unyielding – one surprise after another!

Hu: *Appearing.* My deepest respects, Father. How may I serve you?

Li: *Angry.* By telling me if there's any truth to this story about you kidnapping and beating people!

Hu: Dammit! *Smiling.* Well, there was a very small incident along that line, but – the case has already been disposed of!

Li: Disposed of? How?

Hu: I told the Magistrate that on the day in question, I was studying with scholar Duan.

Li: And – what did the Magistrate do?

Hu: *Chuckles.* He had the old fool who complained beaten to death for wasting his time! Heh heh. The case was settled by eliminating the plaintiff!

Li: *Deeply shocked.* My gods! He beat the man to death! Beaten *to death*? *Pause.* Tell me, did you have a witness?

Hu: Xu Fu was my witness.

Li: *Him*? *To Zhou.* Were you the witness in court?

Zhou: Yes, Lord Xu. *Bowing.* Your humble servant, as always.

Li: Fools! A family slave is not a legal witness in such a case! *To Hu.* You bungling idiot! This affair has been reported to Governor Hai Rui!

Hu: So it costs us a little gold! With the officials in Jiangnan, money solves everything.

Li: Thick-headed dolt! You leapt right into the dung-pile this time. This Governor is not like the others! Damn his eyes! He is more righteous than a lion. In fact, we used to call him "Unyielding!"

Hu: *Relieved.* Oh, well – you *know* him.

Li: I do indeed. And if he investigates this case, you could get a *severe* punishment. He is a dragon!

Hu: *Alarmed.* But Father, what'll we do? Please –

Li: Ha! A bit late for that, isn't it? Even Confucius could not save this situation! *Pause.* Hm, let's see – no. Hm, well – perhaps. Now, I am assuming that you are not as guilty as the peasants say, and that you are truly repentant for what you've done!

Hu: Of course, Father!

Li: A man with a thousand friends has a thousand answers to his problems. And I once did Hai Rui a great service. Come to my study and I will explain what to do. First, you will find Scholar Duan. . . .

They go off.

Lin: The case of Hong Alan versus Xu Ying. The magistrates of Suzhou and Huating will stand before the Governor.

Bi and Chang enter.

Bi: Now I can see how reactionary this play is! I demand that we halt for political discussion.

Feng: At last! Step out here and make your criticism.

The cast comes out on stage.

Lin: What is your objection, Comrade?

Bi: Obvious! All these characters are pre-revolutionary. Ghosts and monsters!

Feng: The landlord and his brat should be liquidated!

Lin: Don't be stupid. You're falling into his trap! Of course they'll be punished! That's the point. That this "saviour of the people" will put them in their place. No need for the masses to rise in revolt! Right – Professor?

Wu Han: I like the suggestions, of course. Would you like a peasant revolt inserted at this point? Comrade?

Lin: Your sarcasm only serves to tie the noose – comrade. The drama will proceed! *Takes her place.*

The case of Hong Alan versus Xu Ying! The magistrates of Suzhou and Huating will stand before the Governor.

Bi: I can't help it, I'm worried. Why did he summon us here?

Chang: I've been on pins and needles for a week!

Bi: He keeps his door shut, refusing to see any officials! And when he goes out, he only speaks to peasants and other riff-raff! What does it mean?

Chang: How could we know he'd slip into the city, wearing a disguise? It's not our fault! We *tried* to welcome him! Now everything's confused.

Bi: It makes a person nervous!

Wu Han enters, in the robes of Hai Rui.

Lin: Lord Hai Rui, Governor of Jiangnan Province. Court is now in session!

Bi: We are pleased to report to Your Lordship.

Chang: We beg your pardon for not meeting you at the gates.

They kowtow together.

Bi and Chang: We beg Your Lordship's forgiveness.

Wu Han: Ah, but we did meet, gentlemen.

Bi: We met?

Chang: Where, Your Lordship?

Wu Han: Come closer, and recognize the "old fool" you pushed into the dust!

Bi: What?

Chang: Who? *Comes closer.* Oh, no!

Wu Han: Tell me – how do you conduct your offices?

Bi: We are absolutely honest!

Chang: And careful!

Bi: We always act in the interests of the Emperor.

Chang: We lift the burdens from the backs of the people.

Wu Han: This is wonderful. Absolutely honest! And you lift the peasants' burdens?

Bi and Chang: Of course, Your Lordship!

Wu Han: How re-assuring. And since you are both so honest, I would like your frank opinions on a contested case. Which is the magistrate of Huating?

Bi: Me, Your Lordship.

Wu Han: How did you handle the complaint of Hong Alan?

Bi: That complaint? Well, I – I handled it with justice! It has already been disposed of, Your Lordship!

Wu Han: And how was it "disposed of?"

Bi: This Hong Alan made wild accusations against Third Master Xu, of the former Prime Minister's family. But when I spoke to the accused, he had a clear-cut alibi. He was studying philosophy! Now, this kind of slander has, quite frankly, been a problem in Huating, Your Lordship – so I threw it out of court.

Wu Han: And who corroborated Xu Ying's testimony?

Bi: The Xu family servant.

Wu Han: A bond slave? I see. *Pause*. And finally I want to know – how did Zhao Youshan die?

Bi: Why – why, it happened as the court bailiff was giving him a few strokes of the cane. Very light strokes, really. . . . How could we know he was old and feeble and would succumb just like that?

Wu Han: Ha ha. Succumb just like that! How very well expressed. Well, I am glad this affair was handled with such strict justice. I think we can proceed. Bailiff! Summon the principals to court.

Lin: *Announcing*. Hong Alan! Xu Ying!

Tang and Hu enter, along with Peasants

Tang: Please, Your Worship. No more punishment! I only wanted justice.

Wu Han: All you have to do is tell the truth. Are these your witnesses?

Tang: Yes. They've agreed to stand with me.

Wu Han: Speak.

Tang: *Sings.*

> I tremble when I face the court,
> So much bitterness is in my heart.
> That tyrant stole my husband's land!
> The loss tore his soul apart.
> That monster took my only daughter;
> He had my aged father caned.
> And when we complained, those judges
> Had my father beaten again!

Musical break.

This time they sent him to his death.

Bi: What lies!

Wu Han: Thank you, Hong Alan. Xu Ying.

Hu: I am here.

Wu Han: This woman has accused you of terrible crimes. What do you say?

Hu: On the day of this alleged offence, I was here in Suzhou! I've brought Scholar Duan here as my witness. But My Lord, this case has already been judged by Magistrate Wang. If you respect my father, don't believe these peasants.

Wu Han: Produce your witness.

Hu: But of course, if the evidence should go against me, I will – according to noble tradition – accept the punishment voluntarily.

Wu Han: *Writing.* I note that you will accept punishment should your evidence prove false. Please call Scholar Duan.

Lin: Scholar Duan!

Zhou appears as Xu Fu, *disguised behind a flowing beard.*

Zhou: Here I am.

Wu Han: You agreed to tell the truth?

Zhou: Yes, indeed.

Wu Han: Was Xu Ying at your home discussing philosophy during the Chingming Festival?

Zhou: *Emphatically.* That is the absolute truth!

Wu Han: Good. And on that day, did Third Master Xu – do anything else?

Zhou: Else? No, no! Well, let's see, he also – wrote an essay.

Wu Han: Ah, an essay! And what was the subject?

Zhou: What? The subject? Of the essay? Let me see, I think it was

– "The Thousand Character Essay."

Wu Han: *What?*

Zhou: *Flustered.* No, no! It was "The Hundred Family Surnames!"

Hu: *Shut up – you imbecile!*

Wu Han: Scoundrel! Impersonating a scholar!

Zhou: Who? I wouldn't dare! I'm not an imposter! I am real!

Wu Han: Oho! Will you brazen it out? And when did you enter the Academy – Scholar Duan?

Zhou: Why – let me think – it was – it was –

Hu: If I may assist the court, I can testify that he really is a scholar – though not well-known – from the District Academy.

Wu Han: Is there anyone here from the Academy?

Chang: *Pause.* I am, Lord Hai.

Wu Han: Ah – Li Pingdu. Are these man's credentials genuine? Think carefully, Prefect.

Hu tries to influence Chang, but Chang's courage fails.

Chang: No, Your Lordship. He is not from the Academy.

Wu Han: *So!*

Zhou falls to the floor and begins to kowtow violently.

Wu Han: *In a rage.* The brass you villains have! Impersonating scholars! Lies upon lies, more suffering to the innocent! Attendant! Remove this cur and flog him to death!

Zhou: *Screeching.* Mercy! I beg you, spare my life! I'm sorry! I'll tell the truth!

Wu Han: All the truth?

Zhou: Yes, yes! Mercy, I beg you!

Wu Han: If you tell the whole truth, your life may be spared. Who are you?

Zhou: *Removing his beard.* I am Xu Fu – Master Xu's servant. See?

Wu Han: And why are you impersonating a scholar?

Zhou: Master Xu ordered me. *Slapping himself in the face.* Oh, if only I could die!

Wu Han: Now we're getting somewhere. Where did Xu Ying go on the Chingming Festival?

Zhou: To the cemetery on Heng Yun Mountain – for an adventure.

Wu Han: Was this woman's daughter interfered with?

Zhou: Yes sir. The master told me to take her to his house. Later I had to beat her a little when she refused to submit to him.

Wu Han: Where is she now?

Zhou: Locked up in his house.

Wu Han: Why was the old man beaten?

Zhou: Well, he blocked our way, when we were taking the girl!

Wu Han: It was a severe beating?

Zhou: Oh yes! Excellent work, as far as beatings go! He had cuts all over him!

Wu Han: Now tell me, Xu Fu. *Confidentially.* Why could Magistrate Wang find no injuries in his examination?

Zhou: *Eager to please.* Master bribed the prefect and the magistrate. They were paid to deliver the verdict!

Bi and Chang rise, alarmed, looking for escape.

Wu Han: Oh, don't leave, gentlemen. We have only begun our investigation. How much were the bribes?

Zhou: Two hundred gold pieces for the Prefect, three hundred for the Magistrate.

Wu Han: You put it in their hands yourself?

Zhou: Yes, Your Honour.

Wu Han: And Zhao Youshan's death?

Zhou: Magistrate Wang ordered him flogged! That's how we won the case. I swear – it was all very proper!

Wu Han: This is the whole truth?

Zhou: I swear it with my life!

Bi and Chang kowtow, weeping and begging.

Wu Han: *Sings.*

These officials are so avaricious
Their corruption stinks up the court.
They wear robes for only one purpose:
Collecting gold for their own support.
But this is the day of judgment;
The people's will shall rule.
The law will be firm as a mountain
And mercy – the dream of a fool.

Wu Han: *Speaking.* This is my decision.

Percussion.

Wu Han: Li Pingdu!

Chang creeps forward, trembling.

Wu Han: You have been corrupt and dishonest, but at least offered the truth before it was too late. You will be stripped of your position and imprisoned for two years!

Percussion.

Wu Han: Wang Mingyu!

Bi creeps forward.

Wu Han: You received bribes, served crooked justice, and murdered one of your plaintiffs. The law decrees you will be beheaded!

Percussion.

Wu Han: Xu Fu!

Zhou creeps forward.

Wu Han: You impersonated a scholar, lied, and conspired to bribe an official. However, you finally offered honest testimony. You will receive one hundred strokes of the cane – and be banished for three years.

Percussion.

Zhou: You are merciful, Lord Hai! Thank you, thank you!

Wu Han: Xu Ying.

With bravado, Hu steps forward.

Wu Han: I find that you kidnapped this girl, beat a defenceless old man, bribed, lied, and conspired to murder. As the law decrees, you will be strangled to death.

Percussion. Hu staggers, shocked.

Wu Han: And for your crimes against the state, all the property seized by your family will be returned to the peasants. The girl, of course, will be compensated.

Percussion.

Wu Han: Are the sentences fair?

Feng: No, the sentences are not fair!

Wu Han: *Surprised.* What?

Feng: Why is the slave punished? He is only an innocent tool of the landlord class.

Hu: Ridiculous!

Feng: He is a member of the proletariat. He can be re-educated!

Wu Han: But every man, no matter what his class, is responsible for his own actions.

Feng: He was ordered by the evil gentry. If he didn't obey, he would be killed.

Lin: Feng is right. There should be lighter punishment for the slave. Do you agree, Comrades?

Tang, Bi, Chang, Zhou murmur agreement.

Wu Han: Very well. I accept the opinion of the masses. Fifty strokes. One year's banishment. Will that do?

Zhou: Maybe we should set me free!

Lin: No, no – it's a reasonable adjustment. Proceed.

Wu Han gestures. Percussion again.

Wu Han: Are the sentences fair?

Zhou: Thank you, Governor Hai! Thank you!

Hu: Lord Hai, consider my father's reputation. He is an honoured public figure! If you don't spare my life, he will lose face.

Wu Han: Silence! If a "gentleman" tramples the law, his punishment should be *greater* than a peasant's! Take them away!

The four criminals are herded off-stage.

Wu Han: Hong Alan, does this satisfy your complaint?

Tang: In one stroke, His Lordship has restored the people's respect for the law!

Peasants: Long life to Governor Hai!

Wu Han: Will the peasants come forward?

They do.

Wu Han: I issue this public decree. The officials have systematically stolen land from the peasants, under the guise of legal action. Now all the land shall be returned to the people.

First Peasant: An earthquake from heaven!

Second Peasant: Our humble gratitude, Your Lordship.

Wu Han: I must now see to my other duties. I take my leave.

He goes out. Music.

Tang and Peasants: *Singing.*

> Rescued from grief, rescued from taxes.
> Our future has never been so good.
> Our land will once more yield a living.
> We'll have enough clothing and food.

Feng throws down his script and stomps across stage.

Feng: This is sickening! Peasants would not grovel in front of this arrogant official. Peasants do not grovel!

Bi: Disgusting!

Lin: Feng – historical accuracy –

Feng: Damn historical accuracy! The play is an attack on Chairman Mao! I can see that! You can see that!

Tang: What do you mean – an attack on Mao?

Feng: Comrade Lin Biao told us at yesterday's review of Red Guards! It's obvious treachery!

Lin: Perhaps you should explain.

Feng: Are you stupid? This Hai Rui is just a stand-in of the traitor Peng Dehaui! He publicly criticized Chairman Mao at Lushan in 1959! Peng attacked our beloved chairman and the great plan for communizing the land. Just as this scum now pretends to give the land back to the peasants! He said The Great Leap Forward was a failure! He was a liar and a criminal! And Chairman Mao fired him, just as this gangster will be fired! It's as plain as the nose on our face! I am not taking part in this treachery!

He storms out.

Lin: Comrade Feng!

Yao blows a whistle.

Yao: All right everyone. Ten-minutes. Break for tea. Ten minutes.

Lights fade to black.

End of Act Two

Act Three

Lights come up on actors returning to the stage.

Hu: But if it's about General Peng – !

Li: It changes nothing! If the play *was* an allegory – which is not even proven – not everyone agrees that Peng Dehuai is a traitor!

Lin: No? What do you know about Gangster Peng – comrade?

Li: He was one of our greatest heroes. He led the First Army in the Long March. And when he commanded our forces in Korea, he destroyed the American puppets!

Bi: He was an arrogant tyrant! He once slapped Kim II Sung across the face for displeasing him.

Li: Gossip!

Lin: And his attack on Chairman Mao? His criticism of the commune system?

Li: He pointed out the facts. Food production after The Great Leap Forward was half what it had been before! We had liberated the peasants, and they were starving!

Lin: You see. He was a tool of Krushchev and Soviet Revisionism!

Wu Han: For being honest, he was dismissed from office and sent off in disgrace.

Bi: Not for honesty! For putting himself above the people! For trying to restore the landlords to power!

Lin: Peng and his clique were exploiting the famine to get power.

Ning: His clique? Who is his "clique?"

Lin: All of them! Deng Xiao Ping! Liu Shaoqi!

Tang: *Shocked.* The President?

Wu Han: Oh yes. Haven't you heard? The President is now a traitor, too. All the wall-posters proclaim it!

Tang: This is serious, Professor. We never discussed these references to Marshall Peng.

Wu Han: It is all interpretation! If people insist on making these comparisons. . . .

Chang: Maybe it's time – for us – to go home.

Lin: No! We are exposing this man's criminal actions. We will continue until they all come to the light. This "scholar" has fabricated an attack on Comrade Mao Zedong and attempted to whitewash the traitor, Peng Dehuai! The so-called hero of this play is not "Hai Rui!" It is Peng Dehuai!

Wu Han: Nonsense!

Lin: Let the play go on!

Yao: We are proceeding?

Tang: *Troubled.* Apparently.

Wu Han: The only course.

Yao: All right –

Yao goes off. Lights change.

Lin: The house of Governor Hai Rui. Three days later.

Li enters as Xu Jieh.

Li: Everything's in turmoil! If people would just do what they're supposed to! Now, I may not only lose my son, but also my retirement estate!

Li: *Reciting.*

> This meddling Lord Hai has gone mad,
> Upsetting our ancient traditions!
> If I can't appeal to his common sense,
> The state will be torn by sedition!

Wu Han enters as Hai Rui.

Wu Han: Good day, Prime Minister.

Li: Unyielding, you came to visit me a few days ago. Now I return your courtesy.

Wu Han: I am greatly honoured. Please make yourself comfortable.

Li: Thank you.

Wu Han: You appear troubled, old friend. May I help?

Li: *Reciting.*

Lord Hai – this is a special case!
All of my other sons have died.
And of all the children you remember,
Only this one is left by my side.
Surely justice must be tempered with mercy
And some privilege shown to age.

Singing.

In my old age, I lost control,
And my child became a criminal.
I beg you now to offer mercy
And make his sentence minimal.
I hope my friend Lord Hai remembers,
That old ties are meant to be strong.
I will give up my land and wealth,
If my son is allowed to live long.

Wu Han: *Reciting.*

Prime Minister, you speak of love,
The bonds of a son and father.
But what about Hong Alan's family?
What future has her daughter?
Do you know how many orphans
And widows live on your estate?
This case is bigger than one son,
It is a microcosm of the state.

Singing.

He's stolen land! Abducted children!
Wages warfare on the peasants!
Do you say we should ignore the law
When justice turn unpleasant?

Li: But the law is not an iron cage! It is an instrument of justice. *Reciting.*

> Xu Ying has clearly broken the law,
> And my reputation lies in tatters.
> But now I'll compensate his crime
> For his life is all that matters.
> Our laws clearly state that this offence
> Can be pardoned through fines of grain.
> Thus could Hai Rui uphold the law –
> and my son could begin again.

Wu Han: You said yourself, "When the law is broken the offender's sentence cannot be token."

Li: True, true! Very true! And do you remember when I said that? When *I* held power in Beijing! When *you* were rotting in the emperor's prison! Do you remember who went begging for your freedom? Yes, Hai Rui – it was I! *Singing.*

> I put my head in the lion's mouth
> By interceding with the Emperor.
> If it had not been for my pleas
> You would not be here as Governor!

Wu Han: You helped free me from prison on principle, not out of self-interest. My crimes were crimes of loyalty, my only sin was my dedication to the emperor! This is quite different, Xu Jieh. By my calculations, your family has seized over forty thousand acres from the people of Jiangnan. And most of it through the schemes of your son. So it is no longer yours to offer as a bribe. I have issued a decree returning it to the rightful owners. *Singing.*

You gentry are worse than wolves,
The way you tyrannize the meek.
The law of the people has spoken
Against those who prey on the weak!

Li: Forty thousand acres. He threatens to take my land – and carry out the death sentence as well! That is going too far! Now he is making me angry! All right, Unyielding, you are bringing punishment upon yourself. *Reciting.*

The landlord class you now provoke
Will unite and come back stronger.
Enjoy that silk hat while you can.
You won't wear it much longer!

Wu Han: So! You'd like to see my black cap removed, Prime Minister?

Wu Han removes the cap.

Wu Han: You think the symbols of power have power in themselves? Here, Lord Xu – take the cap. If I feared your threats, I would hold onto it for my life. But I am a man, not the Emperor's eunuch. And I will answer to the Emperor.

Li: You won't take friendship into consideration?

Wu Han: I have always taken it into consideration.

Li: There is no way for me to keep my estate?

Wu Han: It is not yours to keep, old friend.

Li: You refuse to mitigate Xu Ying's sentence?

Wu Han: "If there is proof, treat it as demanded by the law."

Li: You will not compromise *one tiny bit*?

Wu Han: I never compromise. I am "Hai the Unyielding." *Reciting.*

There is no mercy in revolution.
And I am only the voice of execution.

Li: *Singing.*

You are also a very foolish man,
Thinking to win the peasants' praise.
You dare to defy the landlord class,
You reject our traditional ways.
You rudely ignore my wise advice.
Now – your career will end in a blaze!

Li exits in a rage, throwing the silk hat on the ground. Wu Han reflects for a moment, then picks it up.

Wu Han: *Singing.*

I must be growing old and frail.
For a moment I nearly relented.
But the very thought of giving in
Was the blow my conscience resented.
My justice may be subverted
And my sentences turned all around,
But Hai Rui's name will still shine bright
When the Emperor's sun has gone down.

He puts the cap back on, and exits.

Bi: *To Lin.* Did you hear that? About the Emperor *going down*?

Lin: I heard.

Bi: If this *is* a political allegory –

Lin: Write it down. *Announcing*: Before the court of Governor Hai Rui. One month later.

Music. Chang enters as Dai Fengxiang, the new Governor.

Chang: *Reciting.*

I am Governor Dai Fengxiang,
Newly appointed to the city Suzhou.
It won't take long to get very rich,
So I'm moving as fast as my body will go!

He waddles upstage. Li enters from opposite side.

Li: *Reciting.*

Here's the new governor, just arrived,
A friend of a friend – looking for land.
After greasing a few connections,
The Emperor agreed to give us a hand.
Now this fellow should have in his bag
The authority of a royal decree.
It's what I need to save my son,
I must greet him with a fee.

They meet upstage. Li passes Chang some money. They enter the gate.

Announcer: His Lordship Governor Hai Rui, at his court.

Wu Han enters with Peasants.

Wu Han: Bring in the condemned prisoners! The day of

retribution is at hand.

Hu and Bi enter, bound with ropes.

Wang Mingyou! Xu Ying! You will be executed at high noon.

Hu and Bi kowtow, begging for mercy.

Hu and Bi: Spare me, Your Lordship! Mercy!

Wu Han: Remove these scoundrels. Let the sentence proceed!

They are taken out. Li and Chang enter hastily.

Li: Stop!

Wu Han: Who cries stop?

Li: This is the new Governor, Dai Fengxiang.

Chang: *Reading from a document.* By decree of his Majesty the Emperor, Governor Hai Rui is dismissed from office!

Wu Han: What is that?

Peasants: What did they say? Dismissed from office!

Li: The Governor has created anarchy and conflict throughout the province. The Emperor had decreed his dismissal.

Chang: Long live Emperor Jia Jing!

Peasants: Long live the Emperor!

Wu Han: Long live the emperor! May I ask the new Governor what crime Hai Rui has committed, to be stripped of rank and retired?

Chang: Oppressing the common folk, and abusing the gentry.

Wu Han: I see. *Glancing at Li.* Before you take up your duties, Governor Dai, here is some advice.

Chang: As you wish.

Wu Han: *Reciting.*

> The scourge of Jiangnan is the gentry,
> They rob the people and strip the land.
> This reign of terror must be halted
> Or the nation will rebel at the Emperor's hand.

Li: Renegade! ***Your*** actions have brought turmoil to the province. Upsetting the ancient traditions! The peasants have no discipline! Crops are not being planted.

Yao: He is right! Anarchy and chaos!

Li: Governor Dai will restore authority! Without order, civilization would collapse!

Wu Han: Without questioning authority, there is no civilization! I uphold the law – and the people support me!

Li: Do they? Unyielding? Look around. They'll support you until the next "good official" comes along. And he is here. *Reciting.*

> Man's place in life is governed
> By the laws of heavenly fate.
> It fractures the law of nature
> For people to alter their state.

Wu Han: *Singing.*

You held power at the Great Court,
The Nation's laws were in your hands.
And now you talk of Confucian ethics
While stealing the peasants' land.
But you won't escape your judgment;
In history there's no hiding place.
I may have lost my black silk cap
As the wheel turns. But I've not lost face.

Li: What an obstinate fool! A slight compromise, and your life could be happy. Now, your very life stands threatened. . . .

Lin: It is noon, Your Lordship. We await the order to execute the sentences.

Li: Sentences?

Chang: What sentences?

Wu Han: *Calmly.* The death sentences of Master Xu Ying and his partner in crime. The decree arrived yesterday.

Li: No! *To Chang.* Do something!

Chang: Order the execution halted!

Wu Han: Order the execution carried out!

Chang: *Shrieking.* The new Governor orders the execution to stop!

Wu Han: The present Governor orders that the execution proceed!

Chang: Lord Hai – you cannot kill them!

Wu Han: I am not killing them. I am pulling the lever of justice.

Chang: I have personal instructions from Emperor Jia Jing! Because of the Prime Minister's long and honourable service to the country, his son is reprieved. It's all legal!

Wu Han: May I see the Emperor's decree?

Chang: I rushed here so fast, I left the courier behind. He'll be along any minute. I order a reprieve!

Wu Han: You have no authority. I hold the Emperor's Great Seal.

Chang: Then hand it over, you fool!

Wu Han: I will hold the Great Seal until the execution is carried out. Then Hai Rui may be dismissed from office.

Li: *Arrest him*! He is defying the Emperor!

Chang can only gesture helplessly at the seal wielded by Wu Han.

Wu Han: Long live the Emperor!

Chang: Has he no fear of death?

Li: He is a madman!

First Peasant: Lord Hai, if you fail – we'll be at their mercy!

Second Peasant: Maybe you should relent – just a little – for the sake of all!

Wu Han: If Hai Rui compromised – his body might live – but his spirit would die. And which has the higher value? Carry out the sentences!

The executions are carried out, to the accompaniment of a musical climax.

Li cries out and falls to the ground. Wu Han offers the Great Seal to Chang. Alarmed, Chang tries to avoid the Seal. Wu Han forces it upon him. Music begins for finale, as cast assembles.

Cast: *Singing.*

Heaven is cold and earth is frozen.
The wind whistles through dead leaves.

Suddenly there is the sound of a mob outside. They are yelling, "Death to Wu Han! Kill the traitor Wu Han!" There is a hammering on the door, of boots and clubs.

Cast: *Singing.*

As this just man leaves his post,
Never to return to this place,
His exile to far Qiung-zhao
Leaves tears on every peasant's face.

Sound of the door breaking in with a crash.

Feng: *Off.* Come on! He's still here!

The actors react to the noise. Feng runs in brandishing his gun. Other Red Guards appear.

Feng: Now! The struggle continues! We will deal with the renegades that would halt the Great Cultural Revolution!

Lin: No, Feng!

Li: What an outrage! I'm going for the soldiers!

Feng: Stay where you are!

As Li heads for the exit, Feng stops him by jamming the pistol against this throat. He clubs Li to the ground.

Feng: The rest of you stand back! Our Red Guards have taken over the university. The army unit has been neutralized. *Crossing to Wu Han.* And now, professor, your moment of truth has come!

Lin: Feng, we will continue the struggle session until he re-moulds his thinking!

Feng points the gun at Lin.

Feng: Now I give the orders. This counter-revolutionary garbage will be crushed! Comrades! Who is with us?

Bi: Down with the rightist clique!

Chang: Long live Chairman Mao!

Feng: Do we need any more evidence to smash this capitalist plot?

Lin: The accusations must come from the workers. It is *they* who must be convinced!

Feng: Well? Who will testify against this fascist criminal?

There is a pause. Everything is in the balance.

Tang: I will speak, comrades.

Wu Han: Tianmei!

Li: Comrade, what are you doing – ?

Tang: My judgment on this play was warped by Professor Wu's sympathy for the people.

Feng: You will tell *him*!

Tang: No doubt your portrayal of the feudal state is accurate.

Zhou: Oh, it was like that, all right. Just twenty years ago!

Tang: But in my opinion this play is counter-revolutionary.

Feng: Now we're getting somewhere. More!

Tang: In the new China, only revolutionary peasants and workers can be our heroes.

Bi: Right! These peasants are all ignorant lackeys of the officials!

Ning: That's not true!

Tang: Second, you glorify an official of the oppressing class. The drama says there's no need for oppressed people to revolt against the system! Hai Rui *prevents* revolution.

Chang: He is an enemy of the people!

Bi: There's no such thing as a good official!

Feng: Worst of all, this play stinks of individualism! It praises power-seeking egoists like the traitor Peng Dehuai!

Lin: Would you agree to that, professor?

Wu Han: Comrade Lin, I am not promoting individualism, I am defending a person's right to act. A person's *duty* to act in the public good.

Lin: The individual is a speck of sand to be swept away in the mighty tide of mass power.

Wu Han: But Chairman Mao Zedong is an individual! Where would the Chinese Revolution be today without a powerful leader at the helm?

Feng: Chairman Mao is an exception!

Wu Han: There are always exceptions! Always errors in judgment. And always the need for criticism!

Tang: There can be no criticism of Chairman Mao!

Wu Han: And why not? Have you learned nothing from this drama?

Lin: I warn you, Professor! You are condemning yourself!

Wu Han: Even the Chairman must listen to people – or he becomes another emperor! Look around! What is happening?

He points to Mao's portrait suspended above them all.

Wu Han: We see image worship! We see infallible authority! We see the beginnings of a new dynasty. That is not the Revolution we fought for!

Feng: Shut up! *Threatens physically. Shut up!*

Ning: Please, Professor Wu!

Lin: Do you accuse Chairman Mao of seeking to be an emperor?

Wu Han: I am saying that loyal criticism is necessary – and justified. Hai Rui was a critic! He was one who dared!

Bi: Get him out of here, before he rots the whole academy!

Wu Han: You can remove me, but my play will survive! Not even an emperor can silence criticism when he's in the grave.

Tang: You are taking a very dangerous line, Wu Han. This is verging on sedition!

Wu Han: I am always willing to be instructed, Tianmei. How would you improve the play?

Tang: In a revolutionary opera, the peasants would never put up with such oppression.

Feng: They would smash the system!

Lin: If Hai Rui were a *true* revolutionary, he would renounce his position, leave his family, and lead the peasants into protracted guerrilla warfare against the ruling classes.

Bi: They would overthrow the Emperor!

Feng: *Overthrow the Emperor?*

Bi claps his hand over his mouth.

Ning: Professor Wu – is that what you're saying?

Wu Han: Of course not! In my play Hai Rui is punished for his criticism!

Feng: *Pointedly.* And executed! Correct?

Tang: But I now see that the play *is* an allegory! It must be stopped!

Feng: You're no better than your bogus hero! With all this "superior man" crap!

Lin: You think you're so superior to the masses that you can put anything over on them.

Tang: Comrades, he tricked up into taking part in this subversion!

Feng: You will face a people's court, traitor!

Feng crosses to seize Wu Han.

Ning: *No*!

She tries to intercede. Feng shoots her.

Feng: No more hysteria! If anyone interferes, I'll shoot to kill!

No reply. Wu Han, Zhou and Yao move to help Ning.

Lin: It's unfortunate. She should have stuck to her studies.

Wu Han: Take me away. Before there is more blood.

Feng: *Here*! Your dunce cap!

He jams a dunce cap on Wu Han's head, and removes him at gun point. At the exit, Wu Han turns.

Wu Han: *Reciting.*

> Fierce-browed, I defy
> A thousand pointing fingers.
> Head-bowed, like a willing ox,
> I serve the children.

Feng hustles him out violently.

Feng: *Off.* Comrades, I've got him! I've captured Wu Han!

Sound of cheers, outside.

Lin: *To Tang.* You will be responsible for re-moulding the thinking of this group, comrade. If they make genuine self-criticism, they will escape punishment. Have her taken to the clinic.

Zhou: Bullies!

Lin: There will be many casualties in this revolution, old man. But the will of the people will prevail. Long live Chairman Mao!

She goes out. Voices off begin to chant: "Long live Chairman Mao!" Li, Bi, Hu, Chang, musicians and students slip out. Zhou and Yao, with Tang, lift Ning to her feet.

Tang: Go home, Uncle Zhou. You must be very tired.

Zhou: No, no! I'll stay and clear up the stage.

Tang and Yao help Ning limp out. When they leave, Zhou starts cleaning up, muttering to himself.

Zhou: *Singing.*

> When old men are treated like dogs,
> Even heaven must be offended.
> My tortured body shall be avenged. . . .

Will you look at that! The best silk scarf, from the wardrobe. *Picking it up.* Nobody gives a damn.

He looks toward the exit, shakes his head.

Zhou: Where it is all headed? Nobody listens. No leadership. *Picks up another piece of costume, puts it against his body.* Not bad. Just when I was getting the hang of it too. Ah well, in the next phase of the Revolution, we'll be up on stage to prance round with the rest of them. Can't be such a bad life, acting. *Wielding his broom like a sword.* It'll be different when the Revolution's won! Much different.

The light fades on Zhou sweeping and muttering to himself as he heads for the exit.

Zhou: Yes, heh, heh. That's the truth. Much different when the Revolution's won.

Lights to black.

The End

Further Reading

Published Plays by Ken Mitchell

"Heroes" in *Five Canadian Plays*, Playwrights Canada, 1978.

"Wheat City," Playwrights Canada, 1972, in *Prairie Performance*, NeWest Press, 1980 and in *Ken Mitchell Country*, Coteau Books, 1984.

"This Train," Playwrights Canada, 1973.

"Little Nooton," *Quarry*, 1979.

Cruel Tears, Pile of Bones, Regina, 1975, and Talonbooks, 1977.

Davin: The Politician, NeWest Press, 1979.

The Shipbuilder, *Canadian Theatre Review*, Winter 1979, and Fifth House Publishers, 1990.

The Great Cultural Revolution, Playwrights Canada, 1980.

Chatauqua Girl, Playwrights Canada, 1982.

Gone the Burning Sun, Playwrights Canada, 1985.

Interviews with Ken Mitchell

For Openers, ed. Alan Twigg, Harbour, 1981.

The Work, Conversations with English-Canadian Playwrights, ed. Robert Wallace and Cynthia Zimmerman, Coach House Press, 1982.

Voices and Visions, ed. Doris Hillis, Coteau Books, 1988.

The Ken Mitchell papers are at the University of Regina Archives.